The 10-Day Dopamine Detox Plan

A Practical Guide to the Art of Dopamine Fasting

Jesse Keith

Table of Contents

Introduction

Are you tired of feeling trapped in the endless cycle of instant gratification and mental fog? It's time to take control of your life and breakfre e from the grip of dopamine overload.

My name is Jesse Keith, and I am the author of *The 10-Day Dopamine Detox Plan*, a comprehensive guide to help you regain mental clarity, declutter your mind, and become the master of your own destiny.

With the increasing prevalence of social media, junk food, and instant gratification, it's easy to fall into the trap of dopamine addiction. I have witnessed firsthand the negative impact of dopamine overload on mental health and productivity. That's why I've made it my mission to sharemy expertise and knowledge with those in need.

I offer a science-backed approach to the dopamine detox, guiding you through every step of the way, from setting goals and creating a support system to mental preparation and the actual detox process. You'll learn about the dangers of addiction, the benefits of reducing dopamine levels, and how to maintain a balanced and fulfilling lifestyle forsust ainedme ntal and emotional health.

The 10-Day Dopamine Detox Plan is specifically designed for individuals struggling with dopamine addiction and excessive screen time. It empowers you with the knowledge and tools to reduce dopamine intake, practice mindfulness, and maintain a balanced and healthy lifestyle.

Throughout the book, you'll gain a better understanding of the science behind dopamine, learn practical tips and techniques for reducing dopamine intake, and discover the benefits of a dopamine detox, such as improved mental clarity, productivity, and physical health. You'll also explore the power of habits in shaping your life and learn how to consciously choose habits that lead to excellence and fulfillment.

The key takeaways from the book include understanding the science of dopamine, identifying sources of excessive dopamine, setting achievable goals and intentions, and incorporating healthy habits into daily life. It will answer common questions such as the sources of excessive dopamine, the benefits of a dopamine detox, practical tips, andt echniques for reducing dopamine, and much more.

In the first few chapters of the book, I dive deep into the science of dopamine and its impact on the brain. By understanding the science behind dopamine, you can gain a better understanding of your own behavior and the reasons why you may be struggling with excessive dopamine intake. From there, I take you through the 10-day dopamine detox plan, starting with mental preparation and goal-setting. I emphasize the importance of creating a supportive environment and setting achievable goals and intentions for the detox process.

Throughout the book, I emphasize the importance of mindfulness and healthy habits for maintaining a balanced and fulfilling lifestyle. I provide practical tips and strategies for reducing dopamine intake in everyday life, such as avoiding social media and junk food and incorporatinghe althy habits such as regular exercise and quality sleep.

The dopamine detox isn't just about mental clarity and productivity—it's your gateway to a healthier, more joyful, and fulfilling life. By reducing our reliance on dopamine, we can not only sharpen our focus and boost our productivity but also improve our physical health and enrich our relationships with others. As Aristotle once said, "We are what we repeatedly do." Excellence, then, is not an act but a habit. By making a habit of conscious self-improvement and choosing the right habits, we can unlock our full potential and achieve greatness in all aspects of our lives. So, embrace this challenge of the 10-day dopamine detox and unlock the path to a more vibrant and purposeful life.

I pose these questions to you: What habits are you currently engaging in that are shaping your life, and are they leading you toward excellence and fulfillment? Are you consciously choosing habits that align with your goals and values, or are you simply going through the motions of your daily routine?

Take a moment to reflect on your daily habits and consider which ones are serving you and which ones are hindering you. Then, ask yourself what changes you can make to cultivate more positive and productive habitst hatalignw ith your vision for a fulfilling life.

Remember that a life well-lived is not measured by the amount of dopamine rushes you experience, but by the quality of your relationships, the fulfillment of your purpose, and the peace of mind you cultivate. With the *10-Day Dopamine Detox Plan*, you can take the firstst ep towards a more intentional and fulfilling life.

Areyoure adytole tgoofins tantgratificationan de mbracelong-te rmh appiness?

Chapter 1:

The Dopamine System—How It Shapes Our Perception and Motivation

Have you ever experienced a rush of pleasure after achieving a goal or receiving a reward? That feeling is attributed to dopamine, a powerful neurotransmitter that plays a vital role in our daily lives. From motivation and reward to addiction and mental health, dopamine profoundlyimpac ts our well-being.

In this chapter, we will delve into the science of dopamine and explore its functions, sources, and effects on the brain and body. We will also examine how our modern lifestyle contributes to excessive dopamine production, addiction, and the dangerous consequences that come with it.

Additionally, we will discuss the benefits of dopamine detox, a practice that can lead to improved productivity, creativity, motivation, and mental clarity. Join me on this fascinating journey as we uncover the mysteries of dopamine and debunk common myths surrounding its detoxification.

The Science of Dopamine

Have you ever wondered why you feel good after eating something delicious or accomplishing a goal? This feeling of pleasure and satisfaction is due to the release of a chemical messenger in our brain called dopamine. In this section, we'll take a closer look at the science ofdopamine andit srole inourdaily live s.

What Is Dopamine and How Does It Work?

Dopamine is the ultimate multitasking neurotransmitter in our brain, responsible for helping us with everything from our mood and attention to learning and memory. Imagine it as a messenger, sprinting around our brain, delivering vital messages to different regions to keep our cognitive and emotional gears turning. When dopamine is released, it's like a key that fits into a specific lock, unlocking the door to a world of possibilities. It triggers a domino effect, activating a chain reaction of signals that unleash a host of cognitive and emotional processes in our brain. It's what makes us feel motivated, inspired, and driven to achieve our goals and keeps us focused and alert in the face of challenges. So, the next time you feel a rush of excitement or satisfaction after completing a task or achieving a goal, you can thank dopamineforbe ingt he little messenger that made it all possible.

Understanding Its Effects on Our Bodies

Dopamine is often referred to as the "pleasure" or "reward" chemical in our brain. It's released when we do things that make us happy, like eating our favorite food or achieving a goal we've been working hard towards. It gives us a sense of satisfaction and motivates us to keep going. For example, imagine you've been working on a project for weeks and you finally finished it. When you get that sense of accomplishment, it's because dopamine is released in your brain.

However, having too little or too much dopamine can have negative effects on our bodies. For example, if you have low dopamine levels, you might feel tired and unmotivated.

On the other hand, if you have too much dopamine, you might feel restless and be more likely to develop addictions or other mental health issues.

The Role of Dopamine in Mental Health

Dopamine plays a significant role in addiction, drug abuse, and other mental illnesses such as schizophrenia and attention-deficit hyperactivity disorder (ADHD) (Osmani et al., n.d.). For example, people with ADHD have been found to have lower levels of dopamine in their brains, which may contribute to their symptoms of inattention andhy peractivity.

Similarly, people with addiction or drug abuse issues have been found to have changes in their dopamine system, which can make it more difficultfort hem to stop using drugs.

Dopamine's Ability to Adapt and Change Over Time

One unique thing about dopamine is that it can change over time. If we repeatedly expose ourselves to certain stimuli, like drugs or addictive behaviors, our brain can become hypersensitive to dopamine, and we start to crave the stimulus even more. This is why addiction can be so difficult to overcome. Our brain becomes wired to want that dopamine rush.

In conclusion, dopamine is an essential chemical in our brain that helps us feel happy and motivated. It affects many aspects of our lives, from mood to movement control. However, it's important to maintain a healthy balance of dopamine in our brains. Too much or too little can cause negative effects on our bodies. Ongoing research is helping us better understand the science of dopamine and how it relates to mental andphy sicalhe alth.

The Dangers of Dopamine Overload: How Modern Lifestyle Can Lead To Addiction

Dopamine is a neurotransmitter that plays a critical role in the brain's reward system (Gibbons, 2019). It is responsible for feelings of pleasure and motivation and is released in response to rewarding stimuli. However, modern lifestyles can lead to excessive dopamine production and addiction, which can have significant negative consequences.

The Cycle of Reward-Seeking Behavior

As someone who loves spending time on social media, I know firsthand how easy it is to get caught up in the cycle of reward-seeking behavior. Every time I receive a notification, my brain releases dopamine, and I feel a rush of pleasure. But as I continue to use social media, I find that I need more and more notifications to experience the same level of pleasure. It's like my brain has developed a tolerance to dopamine, and I'm always searching for the next big reward.

The cycle of reward-seeking behavior is a natural process that occurs in our brain's reward system. This system produces feelings of pleasure and motivation, and dopamine plays a crucial role in this process. When we engage in rewarding activities, such as eating delicious food or receiving a notification on our phones, our brain releases dopamine, which creates a sense of pleasure and motivates us to continue engaging in those activities.

However, when we repeatedly engage in these rewarding activities, our brain can become desensitized to dopamine, leading to tolerance to its effects. As a result, we may need to engage in even more rewarding activities or receive more significant rewards to feel the same level of pleasure that we did initially. This can lead to a vicious cycle of constantly seeking new rewards and engaging in more rewarding activities to achieve the same level of pleasure.

In the case of social media, for example, receiving a notification triggers the release of dopamine, which creates a pleasurable sensation in our brain. Over time, our brains can become desensitized to this reward, leading us to seek out more notifications or more exciting content to achieve the same level of pleasure. This can lead to excessive social media use and even addiction as we become trapped in this cycle of reward-seeking behavior.

Overall, the cycle of reward-seeking behavior is a natural process that occurs in our brains, but it can have negative consequences when it becomes excessive or leads to addiction. By understanding how this cycle works and recognizing when it becomes problematic, we can take steps to prevent dopamine overload and lead healthy, fulfilling lives.

How Dopamine Addiction Can Harm Our Health

Dopamine addiction can significantly affect our physical and mental health. When we engage in activities that trigger the release of dopamine, such as using drugs, alcohol, gambling, or social media, our brains can become dependent on these activities to experience pleasure. Over time, this can lead to a decreased ability to feel pleasure from everyday activities, such as spending time with loved ones or engaging in hobbies we used to enjoy.

Research has shown that individuals who struggle with addiction to drugs, alcohol, or gambling have lower levels of dopamine receptors in their brains (Volkow et al., 2012). This means that they have a diminished ability to experience pleasure from activities that don't involve the release of dopamine.

Several studies have supported the idea that addiction can lead to a decrease in dopamine receptors in the brain. For example, a study published in the Journal of Neuroscience found that individuals with a history of cocaine addiction had lower levels of dopamine receptors in certain brain regions than individuals who had never used cocaine (Nestler, 2005). Another study published in the journal Addiction Biology found that individuals with alcohol addiction had lower levels of dopamine receptors in the striatum, a brain region involved in reward processing and motivation (Volkow et al., 2010). These findings suggest that addiction can alter brain chemistry, decreasing the ability to experience pleasure from non-addictive activities.

In some cases, individuals may experience withdrawal symptoms when they attempt to quit addictive behaviors, such as anxiety, depression, andphy sicalsy mptomslike tremors or nausea.

Moreover, dopamine addiction can also have a significant impact on our mental health. Individuals who struggle with addiction may experience shame, guilt, and hopelessness, leading to anxiety and depression.

Additionally, addiction can interfere with work, relationships, and daily life,le adingt omany ne gative consequences.

Therefore, it is crucial to recognize the dangers of dopamine addiction and seek help if necessary. With the right support and treatment, individuals can overcome addiction and regain their ability to experience pleasure from everyday activities.

The Negative Consequences of Dopamine Addiction

The impact of dopamine addiction can be significant, leading to variousne gative consequences.

Here are some of the negative consequences of dopamine addiction (Volkow et al., 2011):

- **Decreased motivation**: Individuals with dopamine addiction may struggle to find motivation for activities that don't provide an immediate reward. This can lead to difficulties at work or school and a lack of interest in hobbies or other activities.

- **Difficulty concentrating**: Dopamine addiction can also impair an individual's ability to focus and concentrate. This can make it challenging to complete tasks or follow through on commitments.

- **Depression and anxiety**: Individuals with dopamine addiction may experience symptoms of depression and anxiety, such as feelings of sadness, hopelessness, or worry. These symptoms may be related to the negative consequences of addiction or the inability to experience pleasure from everyday activities.

- **Physical health problems**: Some forms of dopamine addiction, such as addiction to drugs or alcohol, can have significant physical health consequences. For example, alcohol addiction can lead to liver damage, while drug addiction can cause harm to the brain and other organs.

Preventing Dopamine Overload and Addiction

It is crucial to recognize the dangers of dopamine overload and take steps to prevent it from occurring. This can involve limiting exposure to highly rewarding stimuli, such as social media, and focusing on more fulfilling activities that provide a sense of accomplishment and satisfaction. With awareness and effort, individuals can avoid the negative consequences of dopamine addiction and lead healthy, fulfillinglive s.

Here are some strategies to prevent dopamine overload and addiction:

- **Set limits on highly rewarding stimuli**: Social media, video games, gambling, and other highly rewarding activities can trigger dopamine release and lead to addiction. Setting limits on time spent on these activities can help prevent dopamine overload. For example, limit social media usage to a specific amount of time each day or avoid using devices at least one hourbe forebe d.

- **Engage in fulfilling activities**: Engaging in activities that provide a sense of accomplishment and satisfaction can help prevent dopamine overload. These activities can be anything that provides a sense of achievement, such as exercise, creative hobbies, volunteering, or learning new skills. Focusing on activities that build self-esteem and a sense of purpose can help prevent the need for excessive dopamine release.

- **Practice mindfulness**: Mindfulness practices, such as meditation and deep breathing exercises, can help regulate dopamine production and prevent addiction. Mindfulness can also increase self-awareness and help individuals recognize when they are experiencing dopamine overload.

- **Practice self-care**: Engaging in self-care activities such as getting enough sleep, eating a healthy diet, and exercising regularly can help regulate dopamine production and prevent addiction (Better Help, 2018). Prioritizing self-care can also help prevent the need for dopamine release as a means of coping with stress or negative emotions.

Dopamine is a critical neurotransmitter that plays a crucial role in many aspects of our lives, from motivation and reward to movement control and mood. However, excessive dopamine production and addiction can have significant negative consequences, leading to mental and physical health problems. By recognizing the dangers of dopamine overload and taking steps to prevent addiction, we can lead healthy, fulfilling lives and avoid the negative consequences of this neurotransmitter.

Understanding Dopamine Detox: An Overview

Dopamine detox has become a buzzword in recent years. Many people are looking for ways to reduce their dependence on external rewards and increase their productivity and focus. In this section, we will examine what dopamine detox is, how it works, and its potential benefits.

What Is Dopamine Detox?

Dopamine detox reduces dopamine levels in the brain by avoiding or minimizing exposure to rewarding stimuli. The goal of a dopamine detox is to reset the brain's reward system, decrease dependency on external rewards, and regain the ability to feel pleasure from everyday activities.

Dopamine Detox 101: A Comprehensive Guide to Resetting Your Brain and Transforming Your Life

While it's essential for our survival, overindulging in dopamine-inducing activities can have negative effects on our health and well-being. That's where dopamine detox comes in—a practice that involves taking a break from activities that trigger a dopamine release, such as videogame s,soc ialme dia,andjunkfoodc onsumption.

By reducing our reliance on these activities, we can free up mental and emotional space to engage in more meaningful and fulfilling experiences. This includes activities that don't trigger a dopamine release, such as reading a book, going for a walk, or spending time in nature. These activities allow us to slow down, reflect, and recharge, leading to greater mental clarity, creativity, and inner peace.

Dopamine detox is not about depriving ourselves of pleasure or enjoyment, but rather finding balance and cultivating healthier habits. It's an opportunity to break free from the vicious cycle of addiction and mindless consumption and connect with our true selves. By taking control of our habits and behaviors, we can unlock our full potential andac hieve greater fulfillment and purpose in our lives.

The length and intensity of a dopamine detox can vary depending on your goals and preferences. Some people may choose to do a dopamine detox for a few hours or a day, while others may choose to do it for several days or even weeks. For the purposes of this guide, your programw illlast 10day s.

Challenge yourself to break free from the habits that hold you back and embrace the beauty of simplicity and mindfulness. Who knows? You mightjust disc overaw holene w world of possibilities and inner peace.

The Benefits of Dopamine Detox

Reducing dopamine levels through a detox can have several benefits, including improved productivity, creativity, motivation, and mental clarity. By resetting the brain's reward system, individuals can become less dependent on external rewards and more focused on their goals andpriorit ies.

Let's take a closer look at some of the benefits of dopamine detoxification:

- **Increased productivity**: By reducing the brain's dependence on external rewards, individuals can become more motivated to achieve their goals and can focus better on tasks that require their attention. This increased focus and motivation can lead to higherproduc tivity levels.

- **Enhanced creativity**: Dopamine detox can help individuals break free from routine and habit, allowing them to explore new ideas and thought patterns. This newfound creativity can help them come up with fresh solutions to old problems or generate new ideas.

- **Improved mental clarity**: By reducing the constant barrage of dopamine triggers, individuals can experience a greater sense of mental clarity and reduced brain fog. This clarity can improve decision-makingandre duce feelings of overwhelm or anxiety.

- **Better mood**: Excessive dopamine production due to constant exposure to rewarding stimuli can lead to mood swings and addiction. Reducing dopamine levels through detox can lead to morest ableandposit ivemoods.

- **Greater pleasure from everyday activities**: Dopamine detox can help individuals regain their ability to feel pleasure from simple things, such as spending time with loved ones, enjoying a good meal, or engaging in a hobby. By resetting the brain's reward system, individuals can experience deeper and more profoundple asurefromt hese activities.

- **Increased self-awareness**: During a dopamine detox, individuals must become more mindful of their thoughts and behaviors, including their reliance on external rewards. This increased self-awareness can help them identify areas where they may be overly dependent on dopamine triggers and develop strategies to reduce this dependence.

- **Reduced risk of addiction**: Dopamine detox can help reduce the risk of addiction by reducing the brain's tolerance to dopamine. This reduced tolerance can help individuals avoid the constant need for dopamine triggers, reducing their likelihood of developing an addiction to drugs, alcohol, or other substances or behaviors.

It's important to note that while dopamine detox can have many potential benefits, it is not a cure-all solution for everyone. The effectiveness of dopamine detox can depend on individual factors such aspe rsonalgoals,life style, and mental health.

Understanding the Role of Dopamine in Our Lives

It's easy to fall into the trap of thinking of dopamine as the enemy, especially when discussing addiction and detoxification. However, dopamineplay sac rucialrole inmany ofourdaily ac tivities.

Commonmy ths about dopamine detoxing include:

- **Dopamine is entirely bad for us**: This is a misconception, as dopamine plays a crucial role in several physiological and psychological processes, including mood, attention, and learning. It's not inherently bad, but excessive production of dopamine due to overstimulation can lead to addiction and other negative impacts.

- **A complete dopamine detox is necessary**: This is not entirely true, and it's even impossible to entirely eliminate dopamine from our lives. The goal of a dopamine detox should be to reduce our exposure to excessive reward stimuli, which can overload our brains and lead to addiction and other negative effects.

- **Dopamine detoxing means eliminating all pleasurable activities**: This is not true, as dopamine is released during pleasurable activities such as exercising, spending time with loved ones, and enjoying hobbies. The focus should be on minimizing our exposure to excessive reward stimuli, such as social media, junk food, and video games, while still engaging in healthy and enjoyable activities.

It's essential to approach dopamine detoxification with a balanced and realistic mindset, understanding that moderation is key.

Why a Balanced Approach Is Key

The idea of a complete dopamine detox is not only unrealistic, but it can also be harmful. Instead, it's crucial to approach dopamine detoxification with a balanced and realistic mindset. By reducing our exposure to excessive reward stimuli, we can reset our brain's reward system, decrease our dependence on external rewards, and rediscover the pleasure in everyday activities.

In conclusion, dopamine plays a crucial role in many aspects of our lives, but excessive dopamine production can lead to addiction and other negative consequences. The key to dopamine detoxification is a balanced approach that involves reducing our exposure to excessive reward stimuli without eliminating dopamine entirely. By doing so, we can reset our brain's reward system, decrease our dependence on external rewards, and rediscover the pleasure in everyday activities. This is exactly what this book will guide you to do—have a healthy dopamine detox, so that you can implement the same strategies whenever you feel you need to.

Now that we've debunked some of the common misconceptions about dopamine detoxification, it's time to explore how to prepare your body and mind for a successful detox. In Chapter 2, we'll delve into the practical steps you can take to reduce your exposure to excessive reward stimuli, support your body's natural detoxification processes, andde velop healthier habits.

Asy oue mbarkont hisjourne y, consider the following question:

What would your life look like if you weren't constantly seeking out external rewards?

Chapter 2:

How to Prepare Your Body and

Mind for the Dopamine Detox

If we constantly stimulate our dopamine levels through activities like social media or binge-watching our favorite Netflix shows, we can become addicted to those activities and feel like we need them to be happy *allth e time.*

Whendow e experience that *dopaminerus h*?

Dopamine is typically released in response to pleasurable experiences or stimuli. For example, exercising can result in the release of dopamine, leading to feelings of accomplishment and happiness. Listening to music we enjoy can stimulate dopamine release, providing us with energy and a sense of upliftment. Similarly, socializing with loved ones or receiving positive feedback can also act as a stimulus for dopamine release, creating feelings of joy and connection. Learning new things or achieving a goal can also trigger dopamine release, resulting in feelings of pride and accomplishment. Finally, experiencing novelty, such as trying a new food or visiting a new place, can provide a sense of adventure and excitement while also releasing dopamine.

But did you know that even seemingly harmless things like caffeine and sugar can interfere with this process?

That's right—caffeine, for instance, stimulates your central nervous system and increases dopamine levels, which can make you feel great in the moment. And sugar has a similar effect, providing a temporary boost in energy and mood. But during a detox, these dopamine-stimulating substances can work against you, preventing you from resetting and recalibrating.

So, if you're ready to give your mind a break from the never-ending reward cycle, it's time to cut back on those dopamine-spiking substances and activities and let your body do its thing.

I'll guide you through the essential steps to get you ready for your dopamine detoxing journey; this is your opportunity to break free from addiction and live a happier, healthier life.

Essential Steps for a Healthier Mind and Body

The following is a step-by-step plan to prepare yourself for the challenge ahead.

Step 1: Assess Your Current Dopamine Intake

Do you spend hours on social media every day? Do you find yourself reaching for junk food whenever you feel stressed or anxious? Do you play video games to disconnect from reality? Take some time to reflect on your habits and behaviors and identify the areas where you may be overindulgingindopamine .

Personally, I tend to lose track of time on social media, and I know that Ine ed to cut back (don't we all?).

Let's explore some actionable steps to help you get started:

- **Keep a journal**: Start by keeping a journal of your daily activities and behaviors. Write down how much time you spend on social media, watching TV, playing video games, etc. This will also help you gain a better understanding of your daily schedule and how you allocate your time. Do you use your time wisely?

- **Monitor your moods**: Pay attention to how you feel before and after engaging in activities that release dopamine. Do you feel a sense of euphoria after binge-watching another episode?

Or perhaps your mood improves ten minutes after that fifth cup of coffee?

- **Use apps to track your screen time**: Several apps can help you track your screen time and identify which apps or websites you spend the most time on. Some popular apps include Moment, RescueTime, and Forest.

- **Take a break**: Take a break from your usual routine for a day or two and see how you feel. If you find it challenging to go without the things that give you that instant feeling of gratification for even a short period of time, it may be a sign that you're more addicted to those sources of dopamine than you initially thought.

Now that we know the root causes of our addictions, we can start setting our intentions for the detox journey.

Step 2: Define *Your Goals and Intentions for the Detox*

After evaluating your current dopamine intake, setting goals and intentions for the detox is essential. Think about why you want to do this and what you hope to achieve.

Here are some practical steps you can use to get clear on what you want to achieve:

- **Write down your reasons for wanting to do the detox**: For example, you might want to be more productive to get more work done or have more time to pursue hobbies and interests. Or you might want to improve your mood to feel happier and more content every day. You might also want to reduce stress levels to feel more relaxed. Whatever your reasons, make sure you're clear about what you hope to gain from the detox and that your expectations are reasonable and achievable.

- **Identify your objectives for the detox**: Think about what changes you want and how you can achieve them. Be specific and realistic with your goals and timeframe, and ensure you know why it's important to you. Do you want to improve your sleep cycle and get more shut-eye? Are you hoping to finally train for that 5K race and get more physical now that you're notsodist racted by your addictions?

- **Divide your goals into more manageable and attainable steps**: It allows you to create a roadmap for yourself and helps you track your progress as you work towards your objectives. For instance, if you aim to reduce screen time by 50%, you may start by identifying your current average daily screen time. Then, you can set a realistic target to decrease gradually, say by 10% each day or every few days, until you reach your desired reduction. You may use screen time tracking apps or timers to help you monitor your progress.

- **Keep a record of your progress**: Writing down your goals and accomplishments will help you stay motivated and focused. You can use a physical notebook or an app on your phone to keep track of your progress. Record your progress as you complete each step and journey through each day. This could include the time you spend on your addiction each day, the number of pages you read in a book, or the distance you ran during your workout. Take a moment to appreciate each and every accomplishment, regardless of how big or small, and let them fuel your motivation to keep moving forward. Embrace each step along the way and celebrate your progress with open arms.

- **Use reminders or notifications on your devices to remind you of your goals and intentions**: You can set reminders on your phone or computer to prompt you to take breaks from your screen, get up and move, or engage in other activities that align with your objectives. For example, if your goal is to reduce your social media use, you can set a reminder to limit your daily use to a certain amount or to check it only during specific times. Or, if you're trying to incorporate more physical activity into your routine, you can set reminders to take a walk orst retch every few hours.

Here are some examples of goals to set:

- **Reduce screen time**: If you spend a lot of time on your phone, computer, or TV, you may want to set a goal of reducing your screen time. This could involve limiting your use of social media, setting specific times of day for checking emails or messages, or taking regular breaks from screens throughout the day.

- **Improve sleep**: If you have trouble sleeping, you may want to focus on improving your sleep hygiene as part of your dopamine detox. This could involve setting a regular sleep schedule, creating a relaxing bedtime routine, and avoiding screens or other stimulating activities before bed.

- **Increase physical activity**: If you're not getting enough exercise, you may want to increase your physical activity during the detox. This could involve starting a new exercise routine, taking regular walks or bike rides, or trying a new sport or activity.

- **Reduce junk food intake**: If you rely on sugary or processed foods for quick energy boosts, you may want to set a goal of reducing your junk food intake during the detox. This could involve cutting back on soda, candy, chips, and other unhealthy snacks and replacing them with healthier options like fruits, vegetables, and whole grains.

- **Improve focus and productivity**: If you struggle with procrastination or difficulty focusing, you may want to aim to improve your focus and productivity during the detox. This could involve using productivity tools like time-blocking or the Pomodoro technique, setting specific daily goals, or creating a dedicated workspace free from distractions.

Remember, your goals and intentions should be tailored to your needs and situation. Are they meaningful to you? Don't compare yourself to others or set unrealistic expectations. Celebrate each small accomplishment along the way and stay focused on yourprogre ss.

Step 3: Build a Support System

Whether it's family, friends, or professionals, having someone to hold you accountable and support you through detox can make all the difference. For example, you may share your goals with a friend or family member who can check in on you regularly and offer encouragement.

Here are some practical steps for creating your support system:

- **Determine the people you would like as part of your network of support**: Think about who in your life would be supportive and non-judgmental during your dopamine detox. This person could be a member of your own family, a close friend,orpe rhapsame ntor.

- **Share your goals with them**: Once you've identified who you want in your support system, share your goals and intentions with them. Be specific about what you hope to achieve and how they can support you.

- **Establish a plan for check-ins**: Decide on a regular check-in schedule with your support system. This could be a weekly phone call or a daily text message exchange. Ensure you're both ont he same page about when and how you'll check-in.

- **Be open and honest**: It's essential to be honest with your support system about your feelings and any challenges you face. They're there to support you and help you overcome obstacles.

Your support system should hold you accountable and provide emotional support and encouragement. They can be a source of motivation when you're feeling tempted to break your detox. It is essential to prioritize the presence of positive influences in your life. Negative or unsupportive people can derail your progress and complicate the detox process.

If you're uncomfortable sharing your goals with someone you know personally, consider joining an online community or support group focused on dopamine detox. These groups can provide a sense of community and accountability, even if you don't know anyone in person.

With the right people in your corner, you'll be better equipped to overcome obstacles and succeed in your journey toward a healthier and happiery ou.

Step 4: Create a Peaceful Environment

Your environment can influence your dopamine levels. Prepare your environment to help reduce addiction by clearing out distractions, decluttering your space, and creating a calming atmosphere. Aim to create a relaxing atmosphere that promotes mental clarity and focus.

Here are some practical tips to help you prepare your environment:

- **Designate a detox space**: Identify a quiet and peaceful area in your home where you can relax and focus on your goals. This could be a meditation corner or a cozy reading nook.

- **Reduce the amount of time you spend in front of your screen**: Think about cutting back on the amount of time you spend using electronic devices. Turn off notifications, limit social media usage, or use screen time tracking apps, as I've mentioned before.

- **Remove triggers**: Identify any environmental triggers that may increase dopamine intake and eliminate them. For example, if you tend to snack on junk food while watching TV, remove the junkfoodorfindahe   althiersnac k.

- **Organize your space**: A cluttered and disorganized environment can increase stress and anxiety, leading to excessive dopamine intake. Consider decluttering your home, organizingy ourbe longings,andc reating a calming atmosphere.

By taking these steps, you can create a peaceful, stress-free environment that supports your journey.

Step 5: Mental Preparation

Getting your mindset right is crucial to a successful dopamine detox. It involves setting positive intentions and managing your expectations for the process.

Here are some practical steps to help with mental preparation for the detox:

- **Create a positive affirmation or mantra**: We'll discuss the power of affirmations in more detail later on, but for now, you can create a simple phrase to repeat to yourself throughout the detox process. For example, "I am in control of my actions and choices" or "I am taking care of myself by reducing my dopamine intake." Creating a positive affirmation or mantra is a simple but effective way to reinforce your commitment to dopamine detox and stay motivated throughout the process. You can say it out loud or silently in your head. The key is to believe in the statement and internalize it. This can help you stay focused, motivated, and positive, even when you face challenges or setbacks.

- **Visualize your success**: When we visualize ourselves achieving our goals, we activate the same neural pathways in our brain that are triggered when we actually accomplish them. This not only boosts our confidence and motivation but also strengthens our belief in ourselves and our abilities. To use visualization, start by imagining yourself achieving your goals in detail. Picture the situation, people, and emotions involved. Try to involve all your senses and make the visualization as vivid as possible. Focus on how you will feel once you've achieved your goal and on the sense of pride and satisfaction that comes with it. By visualizing your success, you are creating a mental blueprint for your brain to follow. This can help you stay focused, motivated, and on track toward your goals. It can also help you overcome obstacles and challenges along the way, as you'll have a clear vision of what you want to achieve and why it's important to you.

- **Reflect on your values and priorities**: By understanding why reducing dopamine intake is important to you and what benefits you hope to gain, you can stay focused on your goals and be more committed to the process. What matters most to you in life? What are your long-term goals and aspirations? Then, consider how reducing your dopamine intake aligns with your values and priorities. For example, if you value mental and physical health, reducing dopamine intake can improve your overall well-being. If you prioritize personal growth and development, reducing dopamine intake can create space for more meaningful experiences and self-reflection. Once you have identified your values and priorities, use them as a source of inspiration to keep you motivated throughout the dopamine detox process. Remember, the dopamine detox process is a personal journey, and the benefits you gain from it will depend ony ourow nvalue sandpriorit ies.

- **Practice self-care**: This is another aspect we'll dive into a bit deeper in a later chapter. But for now, it's important to take care of both your physical and emotional needs to ensure that you are in the best possible state to make positive changes in your life. One way to practice self-care is to prioritize getting enough sleep. Aim for at least 7-8 hours of sleep each night and create a sleep routine that helps you relax and unwind before bed. Another important aspect of self-care during dopamine detox is to nourish your body with nutritious meals. Eating a healthy and balanced diet can help you maintain your energy levels, improve your mood, and support your overall well-being. In addition to taking care of your physical needs, it's important to engage in activities that bring you joy and relaxation. This could be anything from reading a book, taking abat h,orgoingforaw alkinnat ure.

- **Use mindfulness or meditation techniques to help manage any cravings or urges**: Mindfulness is an essential tool for dopamine detox, as it can help you manage any cravings or urges that arise during the process. As the first step in your dopamine detox journey, we'll start by incorporating mindfulness or meditation techniques into your daily routine.

When you feel the urge to engage in behavior that releases dopamine, such as checking social media or reaching for junk food, take a few deep breaths and focus on the present moment. Recognize your feelings and ideas, accept them as they are, and then release them. By practicing mindfulness regularly, you can increase your self-awareness and better manageany cravings or urges that arise.

The goal of a dopamine detox is not to eliminate pleasure from your life altogether, but rather to reset and find more sustainable ways to experience pleasure and reward. By incorporating these tips and strategies into your detox process, you can successfully break the cycle ofdopamine de pendency and live a more fulfilling life.

For me, I always look forward to challenging myself and exploring new hobbies during the detox process. It's exciting to see how my mood and energy levels improve as I reduce my reliance on social media and other dopamine-inducingac tivities.

What benefits are you most excited about?

Chapter 3:

The Importance of Maintaining

Conscious Awareness

In this chapter, we emphasize the importance of mindfulness, and I guide you with the help of practical advice on how to incorporate conscious awareness into your daily routine. The initial three days of the ten-day detox break the reward cycle and connect you with the real world, which means putting down your phone and interacting with your external environment. During this time away from electronics, you will focus on conscious sensory awareness and do meaningful tasks. After the first phase, you will feel renewed, revitalized, and more aware of your surroundings.

What Is Mindfulness?

At its core, mindfulness is a technique that involves paying attention to the present moment in a non-judgmental way (Dent, 2017). By becoming more aware of our thoughts and emotions, we can observe them without getting caught up in them. This can help us regulate our emotions and reduce negative feelings.

Practicing mindfulness has been shown to enhance cognitive abilities, including attention and working memory. One study even found that participants who practiced mindfulness performed better on attention tasks than those who didn't (Davis & Hayes, 2023).

Mindfulness can also have physical benefits. In a study of older adults with sleep disturbances, those who practiced mindfulness had improvedsle ep quality compared to those who didn't.

Although it may seem intimidating to integrate mindfulness into your daily routine, it can be accomplished with simple practices. By intentionally focusing on being present in the moment and gradually incorporating mindfulness into your daily life, you can become a calmer, more centered version of yourself.

The Importance of Being Present and How It Reduces the Need for Instant Gratification

In our modern world, it's easy to get swept away by the constant stream of notifications, emails, and other distractions that come with technology. These distractions can release dopamine in our brains, leading to addictive behavior and a lack of presence in the moment. However, practicing mindfulness can help us reduce the dopamine released from screens and other distractions, allowing us to be more present and focused in our daily lives.

By becoming more aware of our thoughts and emotions, we can regulate our emotions more effectively and reduce negative feelings such as stress, anxiety, and depression (Sutton, 2019). We can also promote positive emotions and overall well-being, leading to increased levels of joy, happiness, and contentment (Crego et al., 2021).

One of the keyways that mindfulness reduces dopamine is by helping us become more aware of our cravings and impulses. When we practice mindfulness, we learn to observe our thoughts and feelings, almost as an outsider looking in, which can help us resist the temptation of checking our phones or engaging in other addictive behaviors.

Additionally, mindfulness can promote the release of other neurotransmitters, such as serotonin and GABA, which have calming andmood- boostinge ffects (Krishnakumar et al., 2015).

By reducing our reliance on dopamine and other addictive behaviors, we can cultivate a greater sense of presence and focus. We can enjoy the moment-to-moment experiences that make life meaningful rather than getting distracted by meaningless impulses.

Practicing Mindful Living

Mindful living can be a straightforward and impactful approach to enhancing the overall quality of our lives.

Breathing intentionally is one of the ways that one may cultivate mindfulness—*mindful breathing*. Taking a few deep breaths and focusing on the sensation of the breath moving in and out of your body can help you become more centered and calm. This technique can be particularly helpful in reducing feelings of anxiety and overwhelm.

Another way to practice becoming mindful is through *mindful eating*. When you eat without distractions, such as a TV or phone, and focus on the food's taste, texture, and smell, you can savor your food and become more aware of your hunger and fullness cues. Eating mindfully can also help you make healthier choices and reduce overeating.

Mindful movement is another way to incorporate conscious awareness into your daily routine. This can include trying different types of yoga, tai chi, or even taking a mindful walk outside. Practicing mindful movement can help you become less stressed and more aware of your body at the same time. It can also help you improve your flexibility, balance, and overall physical health.

Finally, *mindful listening* can be a powerful way to become more present and attentive. By listening to music or a podcast without any distractions, you can focus on the sound and improve your ability to communicate and connect with others.

Areth ere any barriers to cultivating conscious awareness?

Potential Barriers to Mindfulness Practice

Here is a list of potential barriers to practicing and becoming more aware, along with the strategies for overcoming these barriers:

- **Lack of time**: I used to think that I didn't have time for mindfulness practice, but then I realized that I could start with just a few minutes a day. Now, I set aside five minutes each morning to focus on my breath and be present in the moment. Mindfulness practice doesn't need much time. Start with a few minutes daily and gradually increase the time as you feel more comfortable.

- **Difficulty staying focused**: Mindfulness is about observing your thoughts and feelings without judgment, even if they are distractions. Don't worry if your mind wanders during mindfulness practice—this is normal. See the distraction for what it is and bring your focus back to the here and now in a soft, non- judgmental way.

- **Self-criticism**: It's common to feel frustrated or critical of yourself if you don't feel like you're "doing it right." When I first started practicing mindfulness, I was frustrated with my inability to focus. But then I remembered that mindfulness is a skill that takes time and practice to develop. I try to approach my practice with curiosity and kindness rather than judgment.

- **Feeling uncomfortable**: Mindfulness can bring up uncomfortable thoughts or feelings, especially when starting. When practicing mindfulness, I sometimes notice uncomfortable sensations, like tension or tightness. Instead of pushing these sensations away, I observe them with curiosity and compassion. I remind myself that discomfort is a natural part of the process and will pass. If the discomfort becomes too intense, try adjusting your posture, taking a break, and returning to practice when you feel ready.

- **Lack of motivation**: There are days when I don't feel motivated to practice mindfulness, but I try to remind myself of the benefits. Practicing regularly makes me feel calmer and more centered throughout the day. It's a small investment of time that pays off in big ways. Staying motivated with mindfulness practice can be challenging, especially if you don't see immediate results. Try setting a goal or intention for your practice, such as reducing stress or improving focus, and reminding yourself of the benefits whenever you feel unmotivated.

- **Resistance to change**: Some people may resist mindfulness because they are attached to certain thought patterns or behaviors. Remember that mindfulness can help you become more aware of these patterns and make changes if you choose. Start with small steps and be open to the possibility of change.

- **Social stigma**: Mindfulness can sometimes be seen as "woo-woo" or New Age, making some people uncomfortable or hesitant to try it. At first, I hesitated to talk to my friends about my mindfulness practice because I worried they would think it was "weird." But then I noticed how much it was helping me, and I became more comfortable talking about it. I've convinced a few friends to try it for themselves! Remember that mindfulness has been scientifically proven to have numerous mental and physical health benefits, and focus on the positive changes you may experience from practicing (Smith, 2018).

There are many potential barriers to mindfulness practice. Still, with patience, self-compassion, and a willingness to overcome obstacles, you can develop a regular mindfulness practice to improve your overall well-being.

The Action Plan: A Breakdown of Days 1–3

By unplugging from technology and choosing to be conscious and interact with the world around us, we can free ourselves from the constant stimulation and distraction that technology provides and instead connect with our immediate surroundings.

Day 1: Unplugging from Technology

Taking a technology detox is an excellent way to disconnect from the virtual world and reconnect with the real world. A technology detox is when you refrain from using electronic devices and technology in general.

Here's a step-by-step guide for day one:

- **Set a specific day and time for your technology detox**: Choose a day and time that suit you the best, where you can go without any technology for at least 24 hours. Consider a weekend, so you don't have to worry about work emails or phone calls.

- **Inform your friends and family**: Let your friends and family know that you'll be offline during your technology detox. They will know to refrain from contacting you during this time, which will avoid any misunderstandings.

- **Turn off all electronic devices**: This includes your phone, laptop, computer, tablet, and other electronic devices. It's best to remove the temptation to use technology altogether. If you're concerned about missing important calls, you can set up a voicemail or out-of-office message that explains you're on a technology detox.

- **Find alternative activities**: Without technology, you'll have more time to explore other activities. You could read a book, go for a walk, spend time in nature, write in a journal, or socialize with friends face-to-face.

- **Limit your usage**: If you need to use technology for work or other necessary reasons, limit your usage to only what is essential. Keep it brief and focused, then turn off your device andre turn to your technology-free activities.

ReflectonDay1

Here are five questions to reflect on after completing day one of the dopaminede tox:

1. Did you feel any discomfort or anxiety from being disconnected from technology? How did you cope with it?

2. What activities did you engage in without technology? Did you discoverany ne w hobbies or interests?

3. Did you notice any changes in your mood or mental clarity throughout the day?

4. How did your relationships and interactions with others change duringy ourt echnology detox?

5. What did you learn about your relationship with technology andhow it affe cts your daily life?

As you reflect on these questions, remember to be honest with yourself and identify any areas where you can improve. It's normal to feel uncomfortable or challenged when making changes to your routine, but the benefits of a technology detox can be significant.

At the end of day one, you might have found it challenging to disconnect from technology initially, but as the day progressed, you may have found yourself more present in the moment and engaged in new activities. You may have also noticed a sense of calm and relaxation that comes from being disconnected. Overall, day one provided a foundation for the rest of the dopamine detox, encouraging you to be more mindful and present in your daily life.

Day 2: Mindful Sensory Awareness

On day 2 of the dopamine detox, the focus is on becoming more mindful and aware of our sensory experiences. By practicing mindful sensory awareness, you can become more grounded and aware of your surroundings, helping to reduce feelings of anxiety, and stress and makingy oumore capable of breaking freefromt he reward cycle.

I'll provide you with three awareness activities; you can try as many as you like. The focus of today is on fully engaging our senses in these activities.

Here's a breakdown of the exercises you can implement today:

Exercise#1ofDayTwo

Let's start with mindfulness meditation.

- **Find a quiet space**: Choose a quiet space where you won't be disturbed,suc hasaparkoraquie t room.

- **Get comfortable**: Sit or lie down in a comfortable position. Youc anuse ame ditation cushion or blanket if needed.

- **Close your eyes**: Close your eyes and take a few deep breaths to relax and center yourself.

- **Tune in to your senses**: When we direct our attention to our senses, we become more grounded and present in the moment. Starting with the sense of touch is a common technique to help anchorust oourbodie sandsurroundings.

- **Move to your other senses**: Move on to your sense of sight, noticing any colors, shapes, or textures around you. Then, move on to your sense of sound, noticing any sounds in your environment, both near and far. Finally, move on to your sense ofsme llandt aste, noticing any scents or tastes you can detect.

- **Observe without judgment**: As you tune in to your senses, observe your experiences without judgment or analysis. Simply notice what you can sense and allow yourself to fully experience each sensation.

- **Practice for at least 10 minutes**: Try to practice mindful sensory awareness for at least 10 minutes. If you find your thoughts drifting, simply guide your focus back to your present surroundings and reconnect with your senses. Be gentle with yourself and allow the experience to unfold in the present moment.

Exercise#2ofDayTwo

Perhaps you prefer listening to music to awaken your senses. Let's explore some ways to deeply engage with music:

- Choose music, such as classical or instrumental pieces, that has the potential to place you in a state of peace and relaxation.

- Locate a tranquil and cozy spot to either sit or recline where you can unwind without interruptions.

- Close your eyes and focus on the music, allowing it to wash overy ouandc almy ourmind.

- Pay attention to the different instruments and melodies in the music and how they blend to create a peaceful and harmonious sound.

- If you find your mind wandering or becoming distracted, gently redirect your focus back to the music and the present moment.

Exercise#3ofDayTwo

Or, if you're anything like me, you'll quickly find yourself immersed in a thought-provoking piece of poetry or sturdy book. The following pointers can help you focus your senses on the movement:

- Choose a book that interests you and that you can fully immerse yourself in, without any distractions.

- You need to find a spot where you won't be disturbed, where you can stretch out and take it easy, and where you can concentrate on what you're reading.

- Begin by taking a few deep breaths and setting an intention to be fully present and engaged in your reading.

- Read slowly and mindfully, paying attention to the words and the story as it unfolds.

- If your mind starts to wander or you become distracted, gently bring your attention back to the words on the page and the story before you.

Practicing mindful awareness Meditation can be a great way to cultivate a greater sense of present-moment awareness and improve our ability to be fully present in the moment (Todd, 2021). By tuning in to our senses and observing our experiences without judgment or analysis, we can deepen our understanding of ourselves and the world around us. Through regular practice, we can develop the habit of being fully present in the moment, even amidst the busyness of daily life. So, take some time each day to connect with your senses and experience the world in a more mindful way.

ReflectonDay2

Here are five reflection questions for the reader after day 2 of the dopaminede tox:

1. How did you feel after practicing the mindful sensory awareness exercises?

2. Did you notice any changes in your level of stress or anxiety after practicing these exercises?

3. Whichoft he exercises did you find most helpful, and why?

4. Did you find it difficult to stay focused on your senses during the exercises? If so, what helped you to refocus?

5. How can you incorporate mindful sensory awareness into your dailyrout ine to improve your overall well-being?

Overall, day 2 of the dopamine detox was focused on practicing mindful sensory awareness to become more grounded and present. By fully immersing ourselves in our senses, we can reduce feelings of stress and anxiety and break free from the reward cycle. The exercises included mindful awareness meditation, listening to calming music, and reading a book mindfully. Reflecting on our experiences can help us gaingre ater self-awareness and insight into our habits and behaviors.

Day 3: Embracing Stillness

The third day of your technology detox is about finding inner peace ande mbracingst illness.

Here are some practical steps to embrace stillness on the third day:

- **Start your day with a guided meditation or yoga session**: Find a guided meditation or yoga video online or use an app to help you get started. Set aside 10–15 minutes to practice, and ensure you are in a quiet and comfortable space.

- **Spend time in silence**: Choose a peaceful spot where you won't be interrupted, and then set a timer for at least 15–20 minutes. Sit comfortably and focus on your breath, letting go of any thoughts that come up. If you find it challenging to sit in silence, you can try using a guided meditation app or a white noisemac hine to help you relax.

- **Take a relaxing bath or engage in self-care activities**: Pamper yourself by taking a warm bath with soothing essential oils or bath salts, or try other self-care practices like getting a massage,t akinganap,orre adingabook.

- **Practice deep breathing exercises**: Sit comfortably and take slow, deep breaths through your nose. Inhale for four seconds, hold for four seconds, and exhale for four seconds. Repeat for five to ten minutes or until you feel more relaxed.

- **Engage in a creative or mindful activity**: Choose an activity that allows you to focus on the present moment, such as painting, drawing, or coloring. If you don't have any art supplies,y ouc ant ry knitting, sewing, or even baking.

Remember, the goal of embracing stillness is to disconnect from technology and connect with yourself. Take the time to explore different activities and find what works best for you. By the end of the day,y oushouldfe el more relaxed and centered.

ReflectonDay3

Here are five questions to reflect on after day 3:

1. Did you try all of the suggested activities, or did you find one that worked best for you?

2. Did you struggle to find stillness and quiet, or did you embrace it easily?

3. Did you notice any changes in your mood, energy, or mental state after engaging in the activities?

4. Did you find it challenging to disconnect from technology and connect with yourself, or did you feel like it came naturally?

5. How can you incorporate more stillness and mindfulness into your daily routine moving forward?

Throughout day 3, you may have found that embracing stillness was more challenging than you anticipated. However, by following the practical steps suggested and experimenting with different activities, you may have found moments of peace and relaxation. By the end of the day, you may have gained a better understanding of the importance of stillness and mindfulness in your life and how they can help you feel more centered and focused. Reflecting on your experience can help you identify what works for you and motivate you to incorporate more peace and mindfulness into your routine in the future.

Final Thoughts on Mindfulness

Mindfulness can help us become less dependent on dopamine and other addictive behaviors, so we can enjoy meaningful experiences that make life more meaningful. So, take a break from technology and try incorporating mindfulness into your daily routine to experience the manybe nefits of conscious awareness.

As you continue on your path to a healthier, more balanced lifestyle, it's important to understand why we also need a physical detox. We'll concentrate on the fourth, fifth, and sixth days of your detox, when you might start to notice and feel some significant changes in your bodyandmind.

Congratulations! You have taken a significant step toward achieving your dopamine detox goals! Are you ready for the next phase?

Chapter 4:

Why Physical Detox Is Necessary

Taking care of our physical health is critical for general well-being, which is why we'll look at why the physical element of this dopamine detox is vital and how to go about it in this chapter.

Let's face it, life may get hectic at times, and as a result, we sometimes forget to pay more attention to the needs of our bodies. We may counteract these impacts, though, by including regular exercise in our daily regimen. Running, cycling, yoga, and weight training can all help balance dopamine levels in the brain, resulting in a more stable and positivemindse t.

Yet exercise is only one component of the puzzle. A nutrient-dense diet is also important for regulating dopamine levels and improving overall health. Getting enough sleep is crucial for physical and mental health (NIH, 2017). A healthy sleep routine can balance cortisol levels, managest ress, and reduce cravings for unhealthy foods.

Therefore, let's get started on a plan of action for physical detox! Day 4 is all about connecting with nature and moving mindfully. Day 5 focuses on cultivating healthy social connections, while Day 6 stresses mindful consumption habits. You may feel more energized, focused, and balanced if you follow these practical measures and integrate them intoy ourdaily rout ine.

Importance of Exercise for Reducing Dopamine Levels

The benefits of exercise go beyond just physical health, and research has shown that exercise is one of the most effective ways to reduce dopamine levels in the brain. When we exercise, our bodies release endorphins, which are natural mood boosters that can help counteract the effects of dopamine. These endorphins also give us a sense of euphoria and happiness that can help us feel more motivated and energized.

But the benefits of exercise don't stop there. It can also improve sleep quality, which can have an even greater impact on our dopamine levels—a good night's sleep can help regulate the levels of dopamine in the brain and keep us feeling balanced and focused.

Many different types of exercise can be beneficial for reducing dopamine levels. Here is an overview of the types of exercises we can dot ohe lpusfe el more balanced:

- Cardiovascular exercises, such as running, cycling, or swimming, boost endorphins and improve overall fitness.

- Resistance training activities, like weightlifting or bodyweight exercises, are effective ways to increase muscle mass and enhance your body's overall composition.

- Yoga and other mindfulness-based exercises can also reduce stress and promote relaxation.

The key is finding an exercise routine that works for you and that you enjoy.

So next time you're feeling anxious or overwhelmed, why not try going for a jog, hitting the gym, or running? Exercise can be a powerful tool for reducing dopamine levels and improving our mental health and well-being.

The Benefits of a Healthy Diet for Dopamine Detox

The foods you eat can significantly impact dopamine levels in the brain, and making simple changes to your diet can make a big difference. In this section, we'll explore the benefits of a healthy diet for dopamine detox and provide practical tips on how to incorporate whole,nut rient-dense foods into your diet.

Research suggests that a diet rich in antioxidants, such as vitamins C and E, can also reduce dopamine levels and improve overall brain function. Some foods that are high in antioxidants include berries, dark chocolate (with at least 70% cocoa), leafy greens, nuts, such as almonds andw alnuts,andse eds, such as chia and flax seeds (Vogel, 2019).

When it comes to reducing dopamine levels through diet, there are a few key considerations to keep in mind (Vogel, 2019):

- **Avoid processed and sugary foods**: Processed foods and sugary drinks can lead to spikes in dopamine levels, which can perpetuate the cycle of addiction. Try to limit your intake of these types of foods and drinks as much as possible.

- **Focus on whole foods**: Eating a diet rich in whole foods can help decrease dopamine levels and promote overall health. Examples of these nutrient-rich foods include fruits, vegetables, several lean proteins, and healthy fats.

- **Incorporate leafy greens**: Leafy greens like spinach and kale are packed with nutrients and antioxidants that can help reduce inflammation and promote brain health. Moreover, they contain high amounts of dietary fiber, which can assist in regulating blood sugar levels and minimizing the desire for high-sugar foods—sonomore snac kingonsugary de lights!

- **Add berries to your diet**: Berries like blueberries, strawberries, and raspberries are high in antioxidants and other nutrients that can help reduce inflammation and promote brain health. They're also a great source of fiber, which can help regulate bloodsugarle vels and reduce cravings for sugary foods.

- **Choose lean proteins**: Eating lean proteins like chicken, turkey, fish, and legumes can help to promote feelings of fullness and reduce cravings for sugary or processed foods (Julson, 2022).

By making small changes to your diet and focusing on whole, nutrient-dense foods, you can help reduce dopamine levels and promote overall health.

StayingHydrated

It's also important to drink plenty of water throughout the day. Dehydration can lead to fatigue, headaches, and other symptoms that can worsen dopamine-related issues (Fletcher, 2021).

Consider these useful suggestions to keep yourself hydrated throughout the day (Migala, 2022):

- **Choose a water bottle you like**: Keep a refillable water bottle with you to increase your chances of drinking water consistently throughout the day. Choose a bottle that you like andfinde asy to carry around.

- **Set reminders**: If you have a hard time remembering to drink water, try setting reminders on your phone or computer to remind you to drink water throughout the day.

- **Drink water with every meal**: Make it a habit to drink a glass of water with every meal. This will not only help you stay hydrated, but it will also help you feel more full and satisfied.

- **Infuse your water with flavor**: If you find water boring, try infusing it with flavor by adding fruits, vegetables, or herbs. Some popular combinations include cucumber and mint, lemon andginge r,orst rawberry and basil.

- **Eat water-rich foods**: If you're feeling thirsty, indulge in some water-rich fruits and vegetables like juicy watermelon, crisp cucumbers, plump tomatoes, and sweet strawberries. Not only are they tasty and refreshing, but they can also help you stay hydrated!

By implementing these simple yet effective tips into your day, you can create an environment and circumstances that encourage you to stay hydrated throughout the day.

In addition to choosing the right foods and drinking enough water, cultivating healthy eating habits is important. We touched on *mindful eating* in Chapter 3; here, we'll discuss the practical ways to implement this healthy habit.

BecomingMoreMindfulofYourEatingHabits

Practicing mindful eating habits is an important aspect of reducing dopamine levels through diet. Mindful eating means being mindful of your body's hunger and fullness signals, taking time to relish and savor each bite, and staying in the present moment while eating (Robinson, 2019).

Here are some practical tips for practicing mindful eating (Robinson, 2019):

- **Listen to your body's signals for hunger and fullness**: Before you start eating, take a moment to assess your hunger level. Are you starving or just mildly hungry? Pay attention to how your body feels as you eat, and stop eating when you feel full.

- **Eat slowly:**Take your time with each bite and savor the flavors and textures of your food. Chewing your food thoroughly can aiddige stion and help you feel more satisfied after a meal.

- **Be present**: Turn off the TV and put away your phone while you eat. This can help you be more present in the moment and fully enjoy your food.

- **Practice gratitude**: Before you eat, take a moment to express gratitude for the food on your plate and the nourishment it providesfory ourbody .

Incorporating these mindful eating habits into your routine can help reduce dopamine levels and promote a healthier relationship with food.

DoesJunkFoodAffectOurDopamineLevels?

So, what's the deal with junk food? Research has shown that consuming high amounts of junk food can alter the brain's reward system, making it less sensitive to dopamine over time (Volkow et al., 2011). This means that individuals who consume a lot of junk food may require even more of it to experience the same pleasurable sensations, leading to a cycle of addiction and unhealthy eating habits.

The study found that a diet high in processed and sugary foods can reduce dopamine receptor availability in the brain, contributing to addictive behavior and other dopamine-related disorders (Volkow et al., 2011). Another study found that rats fed a high-fat diet experienced reduced dopamine release in response to a reward, suggesting that high-fat foods may contribute to dopamine dysregulation (Hryhorczuk et al., 2016).

In addition to altering the brain's reward system, consuming junk food has also been linked to inflammation and oxidative stress (Jiang et al., 2021). Several health concerns can arise due to this, such as obesity, diabetes, and cardiovascular diseases. These conditions can, in turn, worsen dopamine-related issues, such as addiction and depression.

By eliminating junk food from our diet, we can reduce the negative effects on our dopamine levels and overall health. Instead, we can choose to focus on whole, nutrient-dense foods like fruits, vegetables, lean proteins, and healthy fats. These foods provide our bodies with the necessary nutrients to function at their best, without the negative effects of processed and sugary foods.

It's important to remember that making healthy choices is a journey, and we can take small steps to get there. Incorporating one or two healthy food options into our diet each day can make a big difference in the long run. So, let's make a commitment to ourselves to choose healthy options that will nourish our bodies and keep our dopamine levels in check!

Sleep and Its Impact on Dopamine

Getting a good night's sleep is essential for our overall health and well-being, including our dopamine levels. Research has shown that sleep deprivation can have a negative impact on dopamine production and can even increase our risk of developing dopamine-related disorders likeaddic tion and depression (Volkow et al., 2012).

So, how can we ensure we get the restful sleep needed to keep our dopamine levels in check? It starts with creating healthy sleep habits. Here are some tips to consider (NHLBI, 2022):

- **Strive to get 7–9 hours of sleep per night**: To feel refreshed and invigorated, most adults need at least 7–9 hours of sleep each night. Prioritize getting enough rest.

- **Avoid caffeine and alcohol before bedtime**: Both caffeine and alcohol can disrupt your sleep cycle and make it harder to fall asleep. Try to avoid consuming these substances several hoursbe forebe dtime.

- **Create a relaxing sleep environment**: Your bedroom should be peaceful and tranquil. Upgrade your sleep experience with some comfy pillows and a plush mattress, or invest in blackout curtains or a white noise machine to create a peaceful sleep environment that suits you.

- **Keep electronics out of the bedroom**: The blue light emitted by electronic devices like smartphones and tablets can disrupt your body's natural sleep cycle. Try to keep these devices out of the bedroom or limit their use before bedtime.

By prioritizing sleep and creating healthy sleep habits, we can improve our overall health and well-being, including our dopamine levels. Remember, making small changes can have a big impact, so start with one or two habits and work your way up from there. With time and consistency, you'll be on your way to better sleep and better dopamine regulation.

The Action Plan: A Breakdown of Days 4–6

Welcome to days four to six of our physical detox program! In the next three days, we'll be focusing on connecting with nature, nurturing positive social connections, and getting a good night's sleep. By following these practical steps, you can improve your mental and physicalw ell-being and feel more energized and focused.

Day 4: Connecting With Nature—Mindful Movement

Today, we will be exploring the benefits of connecting with nature and engaging in mindful movement. Whether you are surrounded by towering mountains, dense forests, or sprawling fields, spending time in nature can be a rejuvenating experience. It has been proven to reduce stress levels and improve overall mood (Mind, 2021). On the other hand, mindful movement practices like yoga and tai chi have been shown to enhance physical flexibility, balance, and mental well-being (Clark et al., 2015).

Here are some practical steps you can take:

EngageinPhysicalActivitiesThatPromoteMindfulnessand ConnectionWithNature

Starting your day with physical activity is a great way to energize your body and mind. Yoga or hiking in nature are two great options to consider. Yoga can help stretch your muscles and calm your mind before you tackle the rest of the day. If you're new to yoga, try a beginner-friendly sequence, like a gentle flow. Focus on your breath andbe ingpre sent at the moment as you move through each pose.

Here are the steps to complete the morning yoga session:

1. Find a quiet and comfortable space in your home or outdoors where you can practice yoga.

2. Begin with a few minutes of deep breathing to calm your mind andfoc usy ourat tention on your breath.

3. Start with gentle warm-up poses like Cat-Cow, Sun Salutation, orDow nward-facingDog.

4. Move on to standing poses like Warrior II, Triangle Pose, and Tree Pose, which will help stretch your muscles and build strength.

5. Following that, try some seated yoga postures such as Child's Pose, Seated Forward Bend, or Pigeon Pose to extend and loosenupy ourhipsandlow er back.

6. Wrap up your session with calming cooldown postures like Bridge Pose or Legs-Up-The-WallP ose.

Take a few moments to relax in Savasana Pose or seated meditation, allowing your body and mind to fully absorb the benefits of your practice.

Ify oupre fer hiking in nature, here are the steps to follow:

1. Choose a trail or location that suits your level of fitness and experience.

2. Be prepared for the weather and terrain by dressing appropriately, wearing sturdy shoes, and bringing along some water and snacks.

3. Start with a gentle warm-up, like walking on flat ground or doingsome light st retching.

4. Gradually increase the intensity of your hike by including uphill sections or longer distances.

5. Takebre aksw hen needed to rest and enjoy the scenery.

6. When you reach your destination, take a moment to appreciate the view and rest before heading back.

7. End your hike with a cool-down, like walking on flat ground or stretching your muscles.

Listen to your body and adjust your practice or hike as needed to ensure your safety and comfort.

Other physical activities promoting mindfulness and connection with nature can also be beneficial. Taking a dip in a natural body of water can be a revitalizing experience and a great way to feel more connected to nature. It can improve cardiovascular health, muscle strength, and flexibility while reducing stress and anxiety. If swimming isn't an option,c onsidert akingamindfulw   alkt hrought he woods.

As you walk, focus on the sights, sounds, and sensations around you, take deep breaths, and let go of any distractions or worries. Walking in nature can improve mood and cognitive function and reduce stress and anxiety.

The goal of today is not just to perform physical activities but to truly immerse yourself in nature and appreciate the beauty around you. Take some time to be present and notice the small details around you, such as the chirping of birds or the rustling of leaves. These small moments of mindfulness can significantly impact your mental and physical well-being.

ReflectonDay4

Here are five reflection questions to consider after completing day four oft he physical detox program:

1. How did you feel after engaging in physical activities that promote mindfulness and connection with nature?

2. Did you notice any improvements in your mood or stress levels after spending time in nature?

3. How did you enjoy the morning yoga session or hiking in nature?Wasit   challenging or enjoyable for you?

4. Did you feel present and mindful during your physical activities today, or were you distracted by your thoughts?

5. What small details did you notice while immersing yourself in nature today, and how did they make you feel?

Day 4 of the physical detox program focused on the importance of connecting with nature and engaging in mindful movement to improve our mental and physical well-being. By being present during physical activities, we can reduce stress levels, improve our mood, and feel more energized. Taking time to appreciate the beauty around us and noticing the small details can have a significant impact on our well-being. Tomorrow, we will focus on nurturing positive social connections and their impact on our health. Keep up the good work!

Day 5: Nurturing Positive Social Connections

Building and nurturing positive social connections can be incredibly uplifting and beneficial for overall well-being. Day five of the detox is centered around cultivating positive social relationships and limiting exposure to negative influences, including social media and other harmfulfac tors.

Social media can consume much of our time and energy in today's world. However, research has shown that social media use is often associated with negative impacts on mental health, including anxiety, depression, and loneliness (Seabrook et al., 2016). We can improve our mental and emotional health by nurturing positive social connections andre ducingourt imeonsoc ialme diaorw ith negative influences.

Here are practical exercises for nurturing positive social connections (National InstitutesofHe alth,2017) :

- **Schedule time with loved ones**: Make an effort to spend quality time with loved ones, whether having dinner together or planning a fun activity everyone can enjoy. Connect with a friend or family member and schedule a dinner date or movie night together. Alternatively, plan a fun outdoor activity like hiking or going to the beach. If you live far away from your loved ones, you can schedule a video call to catch up and connect.

- **Engage in meaningful conversations**: Instead of small talk, try to have deeper conversations that allow you to connect with others on a more personal level. Spark engaging discussions by asking open-ended questions and showing a genuine interest in what others have to say. Strike up a conversation with a coworker or someone you see regularly but still need to get to know better. Ask questions like, "What do you like to do in your free time?" or "What's something you're passionate about?" Listen actively to their responses and share your interests and passions.

- **Participate in group activities**: Join a community group or club that aligns with your interests and values. Exploring your interests and joining groups or clubs can introduce you to a community of people who share your passions and values, creating opportunities for meaningful connections and new friendships. Join a local book club, sports team, or art class that aligns with your interests. This will allow you to meet new people who share your hobbies and passions and build meaningful connections through shared experiences.

- **Volunteer for a cause you care about**: Giving back to your community can be a great way to meet new people and build meaningful connections. Find a cause that resonates with you and sign up to volunteer your time and talents. Perhaps there is a local charity or organization that aligns with your values; sign up to volunteer your time. This could be anything from helping out at a soup kitchen to joining a beach cleanup crew. Not only will you be positively impacting your community, but you'll also have the opportunity to meet like-minded individuals and build connections through a shared sense of purpose.

Building positive social connections takes time and effort, but the benefits are worth it. By prioritizing meaningful interactions with others and nurturing supportive relationships, you can improve your overallw ell-being and feel more connected to the world around you.

Here are five questions to reflect on after day 5:

1. Who are the loved ones you want to spend more quality time with, and how can you schedule time with them?

2. What are some meaningful conversations you've had recently, andhow didt hey make you feel?

3. What are some community groups or clubs that align with your interests and values, and how can you get involved with them?

4. What organization resonates with you, and how can you make a positiveimpac t?

5. How can you continue to prioritize meaningful interactions with others and nurture supportive relationships in your daily life?

On day 5, the focus was on nurturing positive social connections and reducing time spent on social media or with negative influences. The practical exercises included scheduling time with loved ones, engaging in meaningful conversations, participating in group activities, and volunteering for a cause you care about. Building positive social connections takes time and effort, but the benefits are worth it for our overall well-being and for feeling more connected to the world around us. As we move on to day 6, we shift our focus to cultivating mindful consumption habits and creating a more balanced and fulfilling lifestyle.

Day 6: Mindful Consumption Habits

On day 6 of the detox, the focus is on developing mindful consumption habits. Our daily consumption choices significantly impact the environment and society, and being more mindful of what we consume can have a positive impact. Mindful consumption habits can help reduce waste, promote sustainable practices, and support ethical production and trade (Li et al., 2021). By practicing mindful consumption, we can become more aware of our impact on the world and take small, manageable steps towards more mindful and sustainableliving,fre e from distractions.

Developing mindful consumption habits can be a rewarding and empowering journey towards a healthier lifestyle and a better world. Here are some practical and personal steps you can take today to start your journey:

- **Audit your consumption**: Take some time to reflect on what you consume on a regular basis, such as food, drinks, products, and media. Identify areas where you can make more conscious choices, such as by reducing waste, avoiding single-use plastics, or choosing sustainably produced and ethically sourced products.

- **Plan your meals**: Set aside some time to plan out your meals for the day or week. Adopting meal planning can lead to healthier and more mindful eating habits, reduce food waste, and save you time and money. It's a win-win for both your well-being and your wallet! You can also experiment with new recipes and flavors to make mealtimes more exciting and enjoyable.

- **Practice mindful eating**: Yes! It's worth a mention again. As you become more mindful when you eat, take some deep breaths, and focus on your senses, such as the taste, texture, and aroma of your food. Savor each bite and chew slowly, allowing yourself to fully enjoy and appreciate your meal. This can help you cultivate a healthier relationship with food, reduce overeating, and improve digestion.

- **Reduce screen time**: Set some boundaries around your screen time, such as turning off your phone during meals or before bedtime or limiting your social media use to certain times of the day. By taking a few moments to be present and mindful each day, you can enhance your overall well-being and find a greater sense of calm and balance.

- **Choose sustainable products**: Whenever possible, choose products that are environmentally friendly, socially responsible, and ethically produced. Look for certifications such as Fairtrade, Rainforest Alliance, or USDA Organic, and support local or small-scale producers. By making conscious choices about what you consume, you can support a healthier and more sustainable world.

Developing mindful consumption habits is not about perfection but progress. Every small step you take towards more mindful and sustainable choices counts and can inspire others to do the same. Being kind and compassionate towards yourself and others can create a positiveripple effect that extends far beyond your own life.

ReflectonDay6

From connecting with nature through mindful movement to nurturing positive social connections and practicing mindful consumption habits, each day of the phase is designed to help you achieve a sense of balance and well-being.

Here are five questions for reflection after day 6:

1. What areas of my consumption habits do I want to become more mindful of, and how can I make more conscious choices int hoseare as?

2. How can I plan my meals more effectively to reduce waste and makehe althierc hoices?

3. How can I incorporate more mindful eating practices into my dailyrout ine?

4. What boundaries can I set around my screen time to be more present and mindful in my daily life?

5. How can I prioritize choosing sustainable and ethically produced products in my daily life?

Day 6 of the detox focused on the importance of developing mindful consumption habits to promote sustainability, reduce waste, and support ethical production and trade. By becoming more mindful of what we consume, we can make a positive impact on the environment and society while also improving our own well-being. By taking small, manageable steps towards more mindful and sustainable living, we can create a positive ripple effect that extends far beyond our own lives.

The next step is detoxing the mind and heart; how often do you really check in with yourself? What do you believe to be your source of happiness, and where do you go to get it?

Chapter 5:

Detoxing the Mind and Heart

Here we'll delve into the important topic of detoxifying our thoughts and feelings. It's a common experience to encounter stress, negative thoughts, and emotions in our daily lives, but it's crucial to learn effective ways to manage them without being consumed by them. To live a life free from mindless clutter, it's essential to learn effective ways to manage stress, negative thoughts, and emotions. This chapter will provide you with practical strategies to cleanse your mind and heart, allowing you to achieve inner peace and mental clarity through emotional cleansing.

In the coming days, we'll explore emotional detoxification, cultivating gratitude, and the power of positive thinking. Join me on this journey to achieve inner peace and mental clarity through emotional cleansing.

The Power of Journaling and Self-Reflection

Journaling and expressing our feelings through writing can be powerful tools for self-reflection and emotional release. Not only does it provide a better understanding of our emotions, but it also sheds light on thought patterns and behaviors that may be causing negative emotions. By becoming more self-aware, we can make positive changes in our lives.

Remember that journaling is a personal process, and there is no right or wrong way to do it. Some people prefer to write in the morning to declutter their minds, while others find reflecting on their day before bed helpful to unwind.

When you start journaling, it may feel uncomfortable or difficult at first. However, with time and practice, it can become a valuable tool for self-reflection and emotional processing. Keep at it, and be kind to yourself along the way.

Managing Stress and Negative Thoughts

Stress is a common problem that affects many people. However, there are techniques that we can use to manage it effectively. Some strategies include:

• *Use Positive Affirmations*

Getting started with positive affirmations is simple. Start by taking a moment to check in with your inner dialogue and identify any negative self-talk that may be holding you back. What are some common negative thoughts that you catch yourself thinking?

Once you've identified them, write down a few positive affirmations that counteract those negative thoughts. For example, if you often think, "I'm not good enough," an affirmation could be, "I am worthy oflove andre spect."

Write these affirmations down on a piece of paper or in a journal, and repeat them to yourself throughout the day. You can also create a habit of repeating them at specific times, such as when you wake up or before you go to bed.

• *Practice Time Management*

To get started with time management, begin by creating a list of all the tasks you need to complete. Once you have a comprehensive list, determine which tasks are most important and prioritize them accordingly. For example, if you have a project due next week, that task shouldt akepre cedence over other, less time-sensitive tasks.

Next, assign realistic deadlines to each task and consider how much time each task will take to complete. Don't let overwhelming tasks bring you down. Break them down into smaller, more manageable tasks that you can tackle one step at a time. By taking a gradual approach, you'll be more likely to make progress and feel a sense of accomplishment along the way.

Finally, consider which tasks can be delegated to others or postponed until a later time. Once you've created a plan for managing your time, use a planner or calendar to track your progress and ensure that you're staying on track.

● *Set Boundaries*

Learning to set boundaries can be tough, but it's a crucial part of taking care of yourself. Whether it's saying no to extra commitments or establishing limits with others, setting boundaries helps you prioritize your own well-being and create a healthy balance in your life. Start by reflecting on your own needs and priorities. What activities or tasks are mostimport ant to you?

Once you've identified these, determine what boundaries you need to set to protect your time and energy. For example, if you need uninterrupted time to work on a project, consider setting specific work hoursandc ommunicating them clearly to those around you.

Practice saying "no" when someone asks you to do something that you don't have the time or energy for. This can be challenging, but it's an importantst ep in protecting your own well-being.

Finally, remember that setting boundaries is a process, and it may take time to find the right balance. Be patient with yourself, and remember that you deserve to prioritize your own needs.

Managing stress and negative thoughts is an ongoing process. Don't be too hard on yourself if you slip up or have a bad day. With practice and patience, you can develop habits that promote psychological and emotional well-being.

Positive Self-Talk and Visualization Techniques

The way we talk to ourselves can have a big impact on our mood and behavior. Positive self-talk involves replacing negative thoughts with positive ones (Mead, 2019). Visualization techniques can also help reprogram our minds for positivity and success. Visualizing ourselves achieving our goals can increase our motivation and confidence. When I'm unmotivated, I like to visualize myself completing a task and feeling proud. It helps me stay focused and remember why I'm working towards my goals.

Howdoe s all of this tie into the dopamine detox?

By detoxifying our minds and hearts, we are able to remove any negative patterns of thinking or behavior that may be contributing to our reliance on constant stimulation. When we take a step back and examine our thoughts, feelings, and behaviors, we can gain valuable insightsint oourpat terns and make positive changes for ourselves.

So, what are some practical steps you can take today to detoxify your mind and heart?

The Action Plan: A Breakdown of Days 7–9

Over the next three days, we will explore emotional release, cultivating gratitude, and taking action toward our goals. On day 7, we will focus on freeing ourselves from emotional baggage through self-nurturing, journaling, and practicing emotional regulation techniques. Day 8 will center on cultivating gratitude, a powerful emotion that can help us shift our mindset toward positivity and abundance. Finally, day 9 will be all about taking action and turning our dreams into reality.

Areyoure adytos tartth is journey toward self-improvement and emotional freedom?

Day 7: Emotional Detoxification

Welcome to day 7 of your dopamine detox, where we will focus on emotional detoxification. Today's focus is on freeing yourself from the emotional baggage that can hold you back by taking care of yourself, journaling, and dealing with your feelings. By dealing with your feelings in a healthy way, you will find yourself feeling lighter, more energized, and be tter equipped to handle life's challenges.

Here are some practical ways to get started with your emotional detoxification journey:

1. Journaling

Taking the time to journal and reflect on your emotions can be incredibly beneficial for your mental health and well-being. By writing down your thoughts and experiences, you give yourself the opportunity to process your feelings in a safe and non-judgmental way.

You can gain clarity on what emotions you may be holding onto and why, and even identify patterns or triggers that may be causing these emotions. Journaling also allows you to release any negative emotions that you may be carrying with you, which can help you feel lighter and more energized.

How to get started:

- Set aside 10–15 minutes in your day when you can write without interruptions.

- Finding a writing tool that you love can make all the difference. Whether it's a trusty pen and notebook or a handy digital app, using a tool that you enjoy can make writing more enjoyable and e ffortless.

- Write about any challenging emotions or experiences that you may be holding onto. If you don't know where to start, take a look at the set of questions provided for day 7.

- When you sit down to write, remember that this is your chance to be completely honest with yourself. Don't hold back—the morede tailed and candid you can be, the better.

- Don't stress about grammar or spelling—this is your personal writing space, and there's no one here to judge you. Just let your thoughts spill out onto the page without worrying about getting everything perfect.

Here are some questions to journal on for day 7 of your dopamine detox:

1. What negative emotions or experiences am I holding onto that are weighing me down?

2. Howhave these emotions affected my life so far?

3. How would I feel if I were to let go of these emotions?

4. What steps can I take to release these emotions and move forward?

5. How can I practice self-care to support my emotional detoxification journey?

6. What healthy coping mechanisms can I develop to deal with difficult emotions in the future?

7. How can I create a supportive environment for myself to promote emotional healing and growth?

8. What are some positive statements or affirmations I can say to myself when I feel stressed or overwhelmed?

9. How can I maintain a regular journaling practice to continue my emotional detoxification journey?

10. What can I do today to take care of my emotional well-being andnurt ureamore posit ivemindse t?

Allow yourself to be vulnerable, and don't worry about grammar or spelling. The most important thing is that you take the time to reflect ony oure motionsandgive yourself the space to heal.

2.TakeCareofYourself

Self-care is an essential component of emotional detoxification. Do something that makes you happy and calm, whether it's taking a long bath,goingforaw alkinnat ure,orspe ndingt ime with loved ones.

How to get started:

- Choose an activity that brings you joy and relaxation, such as taking a bubble bath, going for a walk in nature, or listening to your favorite music.

- Set aside at least an hour for this activity.

- During this time, try to be present and fully engage in the activity. Allow yourself to fully enjoy it without any distractions.

3.PracticeEmotionalRegulationTechniques

Learn and practice techniques for regulating your emotions, such as deep breathing exercises, progressive muscle relaxation, and visualization.

How to practice this:

- Choose a technique that resonates with you, such as deep breathing exercises or progressive muscle relaxation.

- Discover a serene and cozy space where you can unwind and relax without any disruptions.

- Set aside about 10 minutes to practice the technique.

- Focus on your breath or the physical sensations in your body as you practice the technique.

4. Identify Triggers

Take note of situations or people that trigger complex emotions in you. This can help you be more aware of your emotional responses and develop strategies for managing them.

How to get started:

- Pay attention to situations or people that trigger adverse emotions in you.

- Write them down in a journal or on one of your note-taking apps.

- Try to identify patterns or commonalities between them.

- Use this information to develop strategies for managing your emotional responses to these triggers.

5. Practice Forgiveness

Let go of resentment and anger by practicing forgiveness. This can be challenging, but it can also be incredibly liberating. Forgiveness doesn't mean condoning harmful behavior but rather letting go of the challenging emotions that can hinder your progress.

How to get started:

- Consider a person or situation you could harbor resentment or anger towards. It could range from a minor annoyance to a long-standing resentment.

- Reflect on why you may be feeling this way. Why does this person or event still have this effect on you?

- Practice forgiveness by acknowledging the hurt and pain they might have caused you but also choosing to let go of the adverse emotions that are holding you back.

6. Reflecton Past Experiences

Take some time to reflect on past experiences that may be contributing to negative emotions. This can help you gain insight into patterns of behavior or thinking that may be holding you back and identify areas for growth and change. Be mindful, and approach this reflection with self-compassion and kindness.

How to get started:

- Set aside 10–15 minutes to reflect on past experiences that may be contributing to difficult emotions.

- Write down any insights or realizations that come up.

- Try to approach this reflection with self-compassion and kindness, acknowledging that past experiences have shaped who you are today but also recognizing that you have the power to change and grow.

By doing things that make you happy and calm and processing and letting go of difficult emotions, you can release complex emotions, cultivate self-awareness, and build resilience for the challenges of life.

Reflecton Day 7

By reflecting on past experiences with self-compassion and kindness, you can gain insight into patterns of behavior or thinking that may be holdingy oubac k.

Here are five questions to reflect on after day 7 of your dopamine detox:

1. What emotions have I identified during my journaling exercise, andhow can I release them?

2. What self-care activities did I engage in today, and how did they makeme fe el?

3. Which emotional regulation techniques worked best for me, andhow can I incorporate them into my daily routine?

4. What triggers have I identified, and what strategies can I use to managemy emotional responses to them?

5. How can I practice forgiveness in my life, and what benefits might this bring?

On day 7 of the dopamine detox, you focused on emotional detoxification. You explored journaling as a tool to identify negative emotions, reflect on their impact, and identify ways to release them. You also engaged in self-care activities, practiced emotional regulation techniques, identified triggers, and practiced forgiveness. The day may have been challenging as you confronted difficult emotions, but it was also liberating as you took steps to let go of negative feelings and cultivate self-awareness. Remember to be patient with yourself, celebrate your progress, and continue to practice self-care and emotional regulation techniques in your daily life.

You can now shift your mindset towards gratitude to cultivate positivity and abundance in your life. It's time to move on to Day 8 and discovert he power of gratitude.

Day 8: Cultivating Gratitude

Welcome to day 8 of your dopamine detox, where we will focus on cultivating gratitude. Gratitude is a powerful emotion that can help you cultivate a positive mindset and attract more positivity into your life. By focusing on the things you are thankful for, you can train your brain to notice the positive aspects of your life, even in the face of challenges or difficulties.

Practical steps to cultivate gratitude:

1. Gratitude Journaling

To get started with gratitude journaling, find a quiet and comfortable space where you can reflect on your day. Set a timer for five to ten minutes and write down three things you're grateful for, big or small.

It's important to be specific and detailed in your descriptions. For example, instead of writing "I'm grateful for my friends," write "I'm grateful for my friends who always listen to and support me."

Try to make this a daily habit, either first thing in the morning or before going to bed.

2. Express Gratitude Towards Others

Make a list of people who have had a positive impact on your life. Choose one person and take a few minutes to write a note expressing your gratitude. It doesn't have to be long or complicated; a simple "thank you" message can go a long way. You can also express gratitude in person, through a phone call, or through video chat.

Take time to express your appreciation for those around you. This could be a simple compliment or a heartfelt expression of gratitude. It can also be helpful to write a letter to someone who has made a positive impact on your life and express your gratitude in detail.

3. Notice the Small Things

Throughout your day, try to be mindful of the small things that bring you joy. Take a moment to pause and appreciate the little things in life. This could be the warmth of the sun on your skin, the smell of fresh coffee, or the sound of birds chirping outside your window. You can also take a picture or make a mental note to remember these small moments.

4. *MakeGratitudeaHabit*

To make gratitude a habit, set aside a specific time each day to reflect on what you're thankful for. Whether it's first thing in the morning or before bed, make gratitude a part of your daily routine. You can also use gratitude prompts or challenges to keep yourself accountable and inspired. Remember, cultivating gratitude takes practice and patience, but the benefits are worth it.

By implementing these practical steps into your daily routine, you'll be able to cultivate a stronger sense of gratitude and positivity. Building new habits takes time, so be patient with yourself and stick with it. Over time, you'll begin to notice the positive impact that gratitude has ony ourw ell-being.

ReflectonDay8

By focusing on the things you are thankful for, you can train your brain to notice the positive aspects of your life, even in the face of challenges ordiffic ulties.

A great way to begin is to start a gratitude journal. Every day, take some time to write down three things that you're thankful for. You can also take a moment to express gratitude towards the people in your life who have positively influenced you. Make an effort to notice and appreciate the small things that bring you joy throughout the day. You can even start a gratitude jar and add a note each day about something you're thankful for. It's a great way to reflect on all the good in your life!

Here are five questions to reflect on after day 8:

1. What are some things in your life that you appreciate and are thankful for?

2. How did expressing gratitude towards others impact your emotions and overall well-being?

3. Did you find it difficult to notice and appreciate the little things throughout the day?Why orw hy not?

4. What are some challenges that you face in cultivating gratitude onadaily basis?How can you overcome these challenges?

5. How do you think cultivating gratitude will benefit your overall well-being in the long term?

Throughout day 8, you focused on cultivating gratitude through various practical steps such as gratitude journaling, expressing gratitude towards others, and noticing the small things that bring you joy. By doing so, you trained your brain to notice the positive aspects of your life and cultivate a positive mindset. You also learned that making gratitude a habit takes practice and patience, but the benefits are worth it. As you move on to day 9, you can take your positive mindset to the next level by exploring the power of positive thinking.

Day 9: Power of Positive Thinking

Positive thinking can have a profound impact on our lives. It can help reduce stress, improve our relationships, and increase our well-being. On day 9 of the dopamine detox, we will focus on the power of positive thinking and how it can help us achieve our goals.

Implementing the steps to harness the power of positive thinking is a straightforward process that requires commitment and intentionality.

Here's how you can implement each step:

1.StartYourDayWithPositiveAffirmations

Begin your day with positive self-talk. Upon awakening, take a few deep breaths and repeat uplifting affirmations to yourself, setting a positive tone for the day ahead. Examples of affirmations include "I am capable of achieving my goals," "I am surrounded by love and positivity," and "I am in control of my thoughts and emotions."

Here are more positive affirmations that can be helpful for overcoming addiction and sticking to the dopamine detox:

- "Iaminc ontrolofmy thoughts and actions."

- "I have the power to overcome my addiction and make positive changes in my life."

- "Eachday ,Iambe coming stronger and more resilient."

- "Iamw orthy of a healthy and happy life, free from addiction."

- "I trust in my ability to overcome this challenge and emerge stronger on the other side."

- "I am capable of resisting temptation and making choices that alignw ith my goals."

- "My commitment to the dopamine detox is strengthening my willpower and self-discipline."

- "I am grateful for the opportunity to break free from addiction andimprove my life ."

- "I am focused on creating a positive and fulfilling life for myself."

- "I am proud of myself for taking this step towards a healthier andhappie rfut ure."

Positive thinking is not just about repeating affirmations; it is also about shifting your mindset towards optimism and focusing on the goodiny ourlife .

2.FocusOnSolutions,NotProblems

When faced with a challenge, try to approach it with a positive mindset. Instead of dwelling on the problem, focus on finding a solution.

- **Reframe negative thoughts**: When you encounter a problem, try to reframe negative thoughts into positive ones. Ask yourself, "What can I do to make this situation better?"

- **Brainstorm solutions**: Instead of dwelling on the problem, you can brainstorm possible solutions and take action toward them.

- **Focus on progress**: Celebrate small wins along the way and focusonmakingprogre sst owards your goals.

Focusing on solutions rather than problems is an essential aspect of positive thinking.

3.EndYourDayWithPositiveThoughts

Before going to bed, reflect on the positive things that happened during the day. Visualize yourself achieving your goals and having a happy,fulfillinglife .

- **Reflect on positive experiences**: Think about the positive experiences you had throughout the day and write them down inagrat itude journal.

- **Visualize success**: Visualize yourself achieving your goals and havingahappy ,fulfillinglife .

- **Let go of negative thoughts**: Release any negative thoughts or worries from the day and focus on positive thoughts before goingt obe d.

Here are some positive thoughts and affirmations you can focus on before going to bed:

- "Iamproudofmy self for the progress I made today."

- "I am grateful for the people and experiences that brought joy to my day."

- "I trust in the journey of life and know that everything will work out for my highest good."

- "Iamde serving of love, happiness, and success."

- "I am in control of my thoughts and emotions, and I choose to focusonposit ivity and growth."

- "I am capable of overcoming any challenges that come my way."

- "I am grateful for the lessons I learned today and look forward to tomorrow's opportunities."

- "Iamsurrounde dby abundanc e and blessings."

- "I am creating a life filled with purpose, passion, and fulfillment."

- "I am at peace with myself and trust in the universe's plan for my life."

4. Identify Negative Thought Patterns

Become aware of negative self-talk and try to reframe those thoughts into more positive ones. For instance, if you find yourself thinking, "I'll never be able to do this," replace it with, "I can do this with practice ande ffort."

- **Identify negative self-talk**: Pay attention to thoughts that come to mind throughout the day and write them down. Identify the more critical thoughts.

- **Challenge these thoughts**: One way to combat negative thoughts is to question their validity and replace them with more positive ones. You can ask yourself if the negative thought is based on fact or is simply an assumption, and if there is evidence to support it. Then, challenge the thought by coming up with a more positive and realistic perspective.

- **Practice positive self-talk**: Practice positive self-talk regularly to rewire your thought patterns.

- **Look for evidence**: When you notice negative self-talk, ask yourself if there is any evidence to support it. Often, negative thoughts are based on assumptions or beliefs that are not actually true.

- **Use logic**: If you're struggling with a negative thought pattern, try to approach it logically. Ask yourself if the thought makes sense and if it's helpful to you.

- **Consider alternative perspectives**: When you're feeling stuck in a negative thought pattern, try to consider alternative perspectives. For example, imagine how a friend might approach the situation or what advice you might give to someone else in your situation.

Why do we struggle with negative thought patterns?

There can be various reasons why people struggle with negative thought patterns, and it may differ from person to person. Here are a few possible explanations (Sage Neuroscience Center, 2021):

- **Learned behavior**: Negative thinking patterns can be learned from our environment and experiences. For example, if you grew up in a household where negative self-talk was common, you might have picked up the habit.

- **Cognitive distortions**: These refer to thoughts that are exaggerated or irrational, leading to negative thinking patterns. These patterns can impact our emotions and behavior. Examples of cognitive distortions include all-or-nothing thinking, which involves thinking in extreme terms such as "always" or "never"; overgeneralization, which involves drawing broad conclusions based on limited experiences; and personalization, which involves taking responsibility for events that are outside of our control.

- **Trauma**: Traumatic experiences can lead to negative thinking patterns, such as feeling hopeless or helpless. For example, if someone experiences a traumatic event like a car accident, they may develop a negative thought pattern that they are always in danger.

- **Depression and anxiety**: When we experience depression or anxiety, it's common to fall into negative thinking patterns. We may see the world through a pessimistic lens and struggle to find hope or joy in our lives. Anxiety can lead us to worry excessively about the future and focus on potential negative outcomes.

It's important to note that negative thought patterns are common and normal to some extent. The key is to focus on finding a healthy balance to combat our irrational thoughts and replace them with something that is true and empowering, and reminds us that we are stronger than we ever thought.

The power of positive thinking is all about creating a positive mindset and focusing on the good in your life. With time, patience, and practice, you can cultivate a positive mindset and increase your overall sense of well-being and happiness.

ReflectonDay9

Here are some questions to reflect on after day 9:

1. What were some positive affirmations that resonated with you andhe lpedy oust art your day on a positive note?

2. Did you find it challenging to reframe negative thoughts into positiveone s?What st rategies did you use to manage this?

3. How did focusing on solutions instead of problems affect your overallmindse t and well-being?

4. Did reflecting on positive experiences and visualizing success before bed improve the quality of your sleep?

5. How do you plan on incorporating the power of positive thinking into your daily routine after the detox is over?

On day 9, you focused on the power of positive thinking and how it can have a significant impact on your overall well-being. By implementing positive affirmations, focusing on solutions instead of problems, and ending your day with positive thoughts, you can cultivate a positive mindset and attract positivity into your life. It may have been challenging at first to reframe negative thoughts, but with practice and consistency, you can shift your thought patterns toward positivity.

Tomorrow, day 10, is the final day of the detox. This is where we bring it all together.

Asy oure flect on the past nine days of this detox, ask yourself:

What is one negative thought pattern that I've let go of during this detox, and how has it impacted my overall well-being?

Chapter 6:

Bringing Everything Together

On day 10 of the dopamine detox, you will spend time reflecting on your journey and the progress made during the past nine days. You will evaluate the changes you have made and celebrate your progress, no matter how small. Then, you will consider how the changes you made during the detox can become a regular part of your daily life, creating sustainable habits that support your goals. You will set specific and achievable goals for continued dopamine detox and create a support system to maintain healthy habits and achieve mental and emotional balance. Overall, Day 10 will be a day of reflection, planning, and self-discovery as you continue on your journey toward a healthier, more balanced life.

Let's jump right in! This is Day 10: Personal reflection and goal-setting.

Reflecting on the Journey and Progress Made

Think about the changes you have made and how they have impacted on your overall well-being. Have you noticed improvements in your mood, energy levels, and focus? Maybe you have discovered new healthy habits, such as meditation, journaling, or exercise, that you want to continue incorporating into your daily routine.

You can further reflect on the emotions and thoughts that arose during the detox. Write down what worked for you and what didn't, and how you can improve your next detox experience. You can also set new goalst hatalignw ith the habits you want to establish in your daily life.

Answer the following questions:

- How have the changes you made during the dopamine detox impacted your overall well-being?

- What improvements have you noticed in your mood, energy levels, and focus?

- Howdidy ouove rcome the obstacles you faced so far?

- Whatdidy oule arnabout yourself during the detox?

- How can you continue to practice reflection and mindfulness in your daily life?

To continue practicing reflection and mindfulness in daily life, it can be helpful to set aside time each day for reflection, whether through journaling, meditation, or another method. It can also be useful to practice gratitude and focus on the positive aspects of life, as well as to prioritize self-care and engage in activities that promote well-being. By staying mindful and reflective, it's possible to continue making progress andimprovingove rallw ell-being.

What did you learn from this experience?

The possible lessons you could have learned up until Day 10 of the detox include:

1. The importance of reflecting on one's progress and celebrating even small improvements in well-being.

2. How to evaluate the changes made during the detox and incorporate sustainable habits into daily life.

3. The benefits of mindfulness, reflection, and gratitude for improvingme ntal and emotional balance.

4. The significance of setting specific and achievable goals for continued dopamine detox.

5. The need to establish a support system to maintain healthy habitsandac hieve goals.

6. The ability to identify which habits to let go of and which to continue is essential for long-term success.

7. The power of self-compassion and forgiveness to embrace the journey and overcome setbacks.

8. The importance of creating enjoyable and rewarding new habits that align with one's long-term goals.

9. The value of setting milestones, tracking progress, and rewarding oneself to stay motivated and hold oneself accountable.

10. The need to avoid old habits that trigger dopamine cravings andmay le adt ore lapse.

Incorporating the Lessons Learned Into Daily Life

Now that you have reflected on your progress, it's time to consider how the changes you made during the dopamine detox can become a regular part of your daily life. Think about the habits you want to continue and the ones you want to let go of.

To get the most out of the detox, it's essential to integrate the changes you made into your daily life. This means creating new habits that align with your long-term goals. For example, if you found that spending time in nature helped you feel more centered and calm, you could make it a daily habit to go for a walk in the park.

Here are some questions you need to consider, with possible answers.

1. **What habits do you want to continue from the dopamine detox,andwhat habit s do you want to let go of?**

   • "I want to continue the habit of reducing distractions andfoc usingonde ep work."

   • "I want to let go of the habit of constantly checking my phone."

2. **How can you start small and gradually incorporate changes into your routine?**

   - "I can start by setting smaller goals and gradually increasing their difficulty over time."

   - "I can also break down large goals into smaller, more manageablest eps."

3. **What plan can you create to incorporate new habits into yourdailylife?**

   - "I can create a daily routine that includes specific times fort he habits I want to incorporate."

   - "I can also use reminders or a habit-tracking app to help me stay on track."

4. **How can you hold yourself accountable for making these changes?**

   - "I can hold myself accountable by tracking my progress andre flecting on my successes and challenges."

   - "I can also seek support from friends, family, or a coach to help me stay motivated and accountable."

5. **How can you practice self-compassion and embrace the journey?**

   - "I can practice self-compassion by reframing negative self-talk and focusing on the positive aspects of my progress."

   - "I can also remind myself that setbacks and mistakes are a natural part of the learning process and that it's okay to take breaks or adjust my goals as needed."

Self-compassion and forgiveness are essential when reflecting on the journey and making changes because they allow us to approach ourselves with kindness, empathy, and understanding. Without self-compassion and forgiveness, we may fall into a cycle of self-criticism, shame, and guilt, which can impede our ability to learn, grow, and makeposit ive changes in our lives.

Can I Make It Last Beyond the 10-Day Plan?

To maintain your progress, it's essential to create sustainable habits for long-term success. This means establishing new habits that support your goals and avoiding old habits that may trigger dopamine cravings andle adt ore lapse.

Consider how you can implement the lessons learned from the detox into your work, social, or personal relationships. For example, if you found that spending time in nature helped you feel more balanced and centered, consider how to incorporate nature into your daily work routine,suc hasby taking a short walk outside during your lunch break.

To create sustainable habits, consider how you can make the new habits you want to establish enjoyable and rewarding. For example, if you want to start a daily exercise routine, find a form of exercise that you enjoy and that is easy to integrate into your schedule. Additionally, consider how you can stay motivated and hold yourself accountable by rewarding yourself for your achievements.

Integrating the Lessons From the Detox Into Daily Life

Integrating the lessons learned from the dopamine detox into different areas of life, we can start by setting boundaries with technology. This may involve setting limits on our screen time, turning off notifications during specific times, or taking regular breaks from social media and other digital distractions. Prioritizing self-care is also crucial, such as getting enough sleep, eating well, and engaging in physical activity. By taking care of ourselves, we can build resilience and reduce stress and anxiety. It also involves developing a sense of awareness and intentionality in our actions. By being intentional, we can live a more fulfilling and purposeful life rather than just going through the motions without direction or purpose. It can also help us avoid feeling overwhelmed or burned out by focusing on what truly matters to us.

In *relationships*, we can practice active listening, which means fully focusing on the person speaking and giving them our full attention. In our personal relationships, we can show empathy by actively listening to our loved ones and trying to understand their point of view.

In the *workplace*, we can also focus on developing our skills and learning new things, which can lead to a sense of fulfillment and motivation. We can also seek out opportunities for growth and development, such as taking on new projects or collaborating with colleagues.

Setting boundaries is also important. This may mean saying "no" to activities or commitments that drain our energy or do not align with our priorities. It can also mean having honest conversations with others about our needs and expectations in the relationship.

In our *leisure time*, we can prioritize activities that bring us joy and fulfillment. This may involve trying new hobbies, spending time in nature, or connecting with friends and loved ones. We can also practice gratitude by reflecting on the positive aspects of our lives and expressing gratitude for the experiences and people that bring us joy. Overall, integrating the lessons learned from the dopamine detox into different areas of life requires a commitment to self-care, mindfulness, andbuildingposit ivere lationshipsw ith ourselves and others.

Integrating the lessons learned from the dopamine detox into different areas of life involves making conscious choices and developing habits that support our well-being and personal growth. By prioritizing self-care, setting boundaries, practicing mindfulness and empathy, and engaging in activities that bring us joy, we can cultivate a sense of balance and fulfillment in all aspects of our lives.

Creating Sustainable Habits for Long-Term Success

To create *sustainable habits*, it's also helpful to start small and gradually build up to more challenging tasks. For example, if your goal is to read for 30 minutes each day, start with 5 or 10 minutes and gradually increase the time each day or week. This approach helps to avoid feeling overwhelmed and increases the likelihood of sticking to the habitint he long run.

To establish new habits that *support your goals*, it's important to identify the "why" behind the habit. Understanding the benefits and purpose of the habit can provide motivation and increase the likelihood of success.

TheImportanceofConsistencyandPersistenceinCreating SustainableHabits

Consistency and persistence are essential in creating sustainable habits to continue the dopamine detox. It takes time and effort to break old habits and form new ones. *Consistency* means committing to a routine or behavior change and sticking to it regularly. It's important to make the change a habit and a part of your daily routine.

Persistence means continuing to make an effort even when it gets difficult or when you may experience setbacks. It's natural to experience setbacks and slip-ups when trying to break old habits, but it's essential to keep trying and not give up.

Both consistency and persistence are important because they help to reinforce the new behaviors and routines that you are trying to establish. Over time, the new behaviors will become second nature, and you will no longer need to think about them consciously. By remaining consistent and persistent, you will be able to create sustainable habits that will help you continue the dopamine detox and lead to lasting change.

Consistency and persistence are crucial in creating sustainable habits forasuc cessful dopamine detox, science agrees, and here's why:

- **Building a new habit takes time**: According to research, it can take anywhere from 18 to 254 days to form a new habit (Lally et al., 2009). During this time, it's important to consistently engage in the desired behavior to ensure it becomes a habit. Without consistency, the behavior may not become ingrained enough to stick.

- **Preventing relapse**: Consistency and persistence also help prevent relapse. It's easy to fall back into old habits if you don't make a conscious effort to consistently engage in new, healthier behaviors (Annual Reviews, 2016).

- **Strengthening neural pathways**: When you consistently engage in a behavior, you strengthen the neural pathways associated with that behavior. Over time, this can make it easier and more automatic to engage in the behavior (Gardner et al., 2012).

Here are some examples of how consistency and persistence are appliedt osust ainingt he dopamine detox (Todd, 2021):

- **Daily meditation**: I'm sure you remember that zen feeling from calming down and focusing on your breath. To make it a sustainable habit, commit to meditating at the same time each day and gradually increase the duration of your meditation practice over time.

- **Exercise routine**: Consistency is key. Commit to exercising at the same time each day, whether it's a morning run or an after-work gym session.

- **Journaling**: Continue with your journaling pursuits! To make it a sustainable habit, commit to journaling for a set amount of time each day, whether it's 10 minutes or an hour. You can also create prompts or use a gratitude journal to keep the habit interesting and engaging.

- **Creative pursuits**: As we know, engaging in creative pursuits like painting, writing, or playing an instrument can be a great way to boost dopamine in a healthy way. Commit to a regular schedule for your creative practice, whether it's a weekly painting class or a daily writing session. You can also set goals orc hallengesfory ourselft oke ep the habit fresh and engaging.

By committing to a routine and gradually increasing your engagement with healthy behaviors, you can rewire your brain and reduce your reliance on unhealthy dopamine-inducingac tivities.

What Are Your Triggers?

Identifying triggers and developing alternative behaviors is an effective way to change and create new habits. By recognizing what triggers our cravings, we can be proactive and take steps to avoid them or find healthier alternatives.

Triggersre lated to the dopamine detox might include (Gillette, 2023):

- **Social media**: Scrolling through social media can be a major trigger for dopamine cravings and distract you from your goals. Consider limiting your use of social media or using a social media blocker to avoid temptation.

- **Junk food**: Eating junk food or consuming sugary drinks can give you a quick dopamine hit but can also lead to unhealthy eating habits. Try to avoid junk food and opt for healthy snacks that will keep you full and satisfied.

- **Gaming or streaming**: Playing video games or binge-watching shows can be enjoyable, but they can also take up a lot of your time and be a major distraction. Consider limiting your time on these activities and finding alternative activities that promote healthy habits.

- **Shopping**: Retail therapy is a real thing, and buying new things can give you a rush of dopamine. During a dopamine detox, consider avoiding shopping or finding alternative ways to reward yourself that don't involve spending money.

- **Our thoughts**: Negative thoughts can be a major trigger for unhealthy behaviors and can lead to a cycle of self-sabotage. Try to focus on positive self-talk and cultivate a sense of self-compassion.

By identifying these triggers and coming up with alternative behaviors, you can create new, healthy habits and make the dopamine detox more effective.

For example, if social media is a trigger for procrastination or negative self-talk, taking a break or using a social media blocker during certain times of the day can be helpful. Instead, you can engage in activities that promote positive self-talk, such as exercise or reading a book. Finding healthy alternatives that you enjoy and can stick to in the long term is essential.

Overall, creating sustainable habits and integrating the lessons from the dopamine detox into different areas of life requires a commitment to self-awareness, intentionality, and self-care. By making conscious choices and developing positive habits, we can cultivate a sense of balance, fulfillment, and success in all aspects of our lives.

Setting Long-Term Goals for Continued Dopamine Detox

As you continue on your journey to reduce dopamine intake, it's important to set long-term goals for continued success. They should align with your values and priorities, and be realistic given your current circumstances.

Think about the habits or behaviors that you would like to change in the long term.

For example, you may want to reduce your social media usage, spend less time watching TV, or decrease your intake of sugary or processed foods. Setting specific and achievable goals will help you stay motivated andc ommitted to your personal growth.

Considert he following set of questions:

- What habits or behaviors do you want to change in the long term?

- What are some ways to establish goals that are both specific andat tainable, while also reflecting your values and priorities?

- How can you make sure your goals are measurable and time-bound?

- What steps can you take to regularly assess your progress and makeadjust ments as needed?

- How can you stay motivated and committed to your personal growth?

To set long-term goals for continued dopamine detox, start by identifying the habits or behaviors that you want to change in the long term. These may include reducing screen time, limiting social media usage, decreasing junk food intake, or reducing time spent on other dopamine-inducingac tivities.

Once you have identified the habits or behaviors you want to change, set specific and achievable goals that align with your values and priorities. For example, you may set a goal to limit social media usage to 30 minutes per day or reduce TV time to no more than two hours per day.

Here are some tips for evaluating progress and setting specific and achievable goals during a detox:

- **Keep a journal**: Writing down how you feel each day can help you track your progress and identify any patterns or changes in your body and mind. You can also write down any goals you want to achieve during the detox and track your progress towards them.

- **Take measurements**: If weight loss is one of your goals, consider taking measurements of your body before and after the detox. This can give you a clear picture of your progress andhe lpy ouse t realistic goals for the future.

- **Monitor your energy levels**: One of the benefits of a detox is increased energy and mental clarity. Take note of how you feel throughout the day and compare it to how you felt before the detox. This can help you evaluate how the detox is impacting your energy levels.

- **Set specific and achievable goals**: To make sure your goals are measurable and time-bound, use the SMART goal-setting framework. Make sure your goals are specific and clearly defined so that you can measure progress and track your success. Set achievable goals that align with your current circumstances and make sure they are relevant to your values and priorities. If you feel unsure of how to set smart goals, skip this part for now; we'll discuss it again in a later section.

- **Celebrate your successes**: Don't forget to celebrate your successes along the way. If you achieve one of your goals, take time to acknowledge and celebrate it. This can help keep you motivated and focused on your overall goal of improving your health and well-being.

- **Write down your goals**: Keep them somewhere visible, like a journal, planner, or sticky note on your computer. By regularly assessing your progress and making adjustments as needed, you can stay accountable and motivated toward achieving your goals. You may find that some goals are easier to achieve than others or that you need to adjust your timeline. Be flexible and willing to adapt as needed.

Creating a Support System and Developing a Positive Mindset

Finally, it's important to create a support system and develop a positive mindset to maintain healthy habits and achieve mental and emotional balance. This may include seeking out the support of friends and family, joining a support group or therapy, practicing self-compassion, andc ultivatinggrat itude and mindfulness.

Answer the following questions:

- How can you create a support system to maintain healthy habitsandac hieve mental and emotional balance?

- From whom can you seek support, such as friends or family members?

- How can you practice self-compassion and kindness towards yourself?

- What strategies can you use to cultivate gratitude and mindfulness?

- What are some practical ways to find an accountability partner who can support and motivate you to achieve your goals?

As you've come to realize, creating a positive support system can be a game-changer. This can involve talking to friends, family, or a therapist about your goals, or even finding an accountability partner who is also interested in making positive changes in their lives. Having a support system, whether it be friends, family, or a professional, can provide encouragement, guidance, and accountability during difficult times.

Final Thoughts

In conclusion, the 10-day dopamine detox is just the beginning of a journey towards a healthier, more balanced life. You can achieve continued personal growth and success by reflecting on your progress, incorporating the lessons learned into your daily life, setting long-term goals, and creating a personal support system. The key to success is consistency, patience, and self-compassion.

Chapter 7:

Sustaining a Dopamine Detox Way of Life

In the previous chapters, we have covered the importance of dopamine detox, how to prepare for it, and how to implement it. Now that you have completed the detox, sustaining the progress made during the detox is essential. This chapter will discuss strategies for sustaining a dopaminede tox lifestyle.

Developing a Long-Term Plan for Dopamine Detox

By having a solid plan in place, you will be better equipped to stay on track and make progress toward your bigger goals.

Setting Long-Term Goals

In Chapter 6, we discussed setting long-term goals for continued dopamine detox. These goals provide direction and purpose for the detox journey. Review these goals and determine if they need to be adjusted to fit your current situation.

To continue living a life free from dopamine addiction, it is important to set SMART goals. Here is an example of a possible SMART goal goingforw ard:

- **Specific:**Iw illlimit my soc ialme diause to one hour per day.

- **Measurable**: I will track my social media use with a time tracker app.

- **Achievable**: This goal is achievable as I have successfully reduced my social media use during the detox.

- **Relevant**: Social media use was one of my biggest sources of dopamineaddic tion.

- **Time-bound:**Iw illac hieve this goal in the next 30 days.

HowcanIre viewmygoals ?

To review your goals for continued dopamine detox, you can start by taking a step back and reflecting on your progress since completing the detox. You can ask yourself questions such as:

- HaveIac hieved the goals I set for myself during the detox?

- Are those goals still relevant to me, or have my priorities changed?

- Have I encountered any new challenges I must address in my goals?

- Have I been able to sustain the progress I made during the detox?

After reflecting on your progress, you can review the original goals and assess whether they need to be adjusted to better align with your current situation and needs.

Identifying Potential Obstacles

Consider the potential obstacles that may arise after completing your dopamine detox journey. Identifying potential obstacles is essential to sustaining a dopamine detox lifestyle. These obstacles can hinder your progressandpre vent you from achieving what you set out to do.

Here are some common potential obstacles you may face and some practical steps you can take to overcome them:

- **Stress**: Stress is a common obstacle that can trigger dopamine cravings. Try practicing mindfulness techniques, such as deep breathing, meditation, or yoga, to overcome stress. Engaging in physical activities, such as running or hiking, can also help reduce stress levels.

- **Social Pressures**: Sometimes, social pressures from our friends or family can be challenging. You may feel pressure to engage in activities that trigger dopamine release, such as going out to eat or drinking a few beers. This might not be in line with your goals. To overcome social pressures, try finding like-minded individualsw hosupport your objectives.

- **Boredom**: Boredom can be a significant trigger for dopamine cravings. To overcome boredom, find new hobbies or activities that you enjoy. Engage in activities that challenge your mind, such as puzzles or reading, and participate in physical activities likesw immingorbiking.

- **Negative Self-Talk**: As we've discussed, negative self-talk can hinder your progress and lead to feelings of self-doubt. To overcome negative self-talk, try practicing positive affirmations, such as "I am capable of achieving my goals" or "I am strong and resilient." Surround yourself with positive influences, such asuplift ingmusic ormot ivationalquot es.

Remember, identifying potential obstacles is the first step in overcoming them. By developing strategies to overcome these obstacles, you can stay on track with your goals and sustain a dopamine detox lifestyle.

Embracing the Journey and Practicing Self-Compassion

The dopamine detox has been challenging, and you've made it. It's time to start preparing for the long term. It is essential to embrace your new objectives and practice self-compassion and kindness towards yourself.

Cultivating a Mindset of Self-Compassion

Recognize that setbacks and challenges are a natural part of the journey. Be gentle with yourself, avoid self-judgment, and develop a self-critical mindset.

What is a self-critical mindset?

A self-critical mindset is when you tend to judge and criticize yourself harshly. You may focus on your flaws and mistakes and have a hard time accepting yourself as you are. This mindset can damage your self-esteem and well-being, leading to feelings of anxiety, depression, and low self-worth. If you have been feeling self-critical lately, you must recognize that you are not alone and that it's possible to shift your mindset to one of self-compassion and kindness. By acknowledging your strengths, focusing on your progress, and treating yourself with empathy and understanding, you can cultivate a more positive and uplifting attitude toward yourself. Remember, you are worthy of love andac ceptance, and it starts with how you treat yourself.

What is a self-compassionate attitude?

Self-compassion is all about being kind to yourself and treating yourself like you would treat a good friend. It means understanding that we are not perfect and that mistakes and setbacks are a natural part of life. Instead of being hard on ourselves, we can be gentle and supportive, allowing ourselves to grow and learn from our experiences. Practicing self-compassion can help us be more resilient, happier, and fulfilled. So be kind to yourself as you embrace this new way of life.

Why is our mindset so crucial for sustaining the dopamine detox way of life?

Our mindset is crucial for sustaining a dopamine detox way of life. When we adopt a positive and accepting mindset, we are better equipped to face setbacks and challenges as natural parts of our journey. Treating ourselves with kindness and understanding creates a moresupport ive environment for growth and learning.

On the other hand, a self-critical mindset can be detrimental to our self-esteem and well-being (Neff, 2011). It can lead to negative emotions like anxiety, depression, and low self-worth, hindering our ability to continue the dopamine detox. We can build resilience and positivity that fuel our progress by shifting our focus to our strengths andac complishments.

Strategies for Coping With Setbacks and Challenges

When setbacks and challenges occur, it can be tempting to give up. Instead, consider strategies for coping with setbacks and challenges.

We've discussed various strategies for coping with life's struggles. The strategies included practicing mindfulness, practicing self-care, connecting with like-minded individuals, being more grateful, and so on.

Here are some other strategies to keep you going as well:

- **Challenge yourself in a new way**: Trying something new and challenging can be a powerful way to build resilience and boost confidence. Whether it's learning a new language, taking a dance class, or trying a new sport, pushing yourself outside of your comfort zone can help you build new skills and gain a sense of accomplishment.

- **Practice acceptance**: Accepting difficult emotions and experiences is an important part of coping with setbacks and challenges. This involves acknowledging and validating your feelings without trying to change or fix them. Acceptance can help you reduce stress and build resilience by allowing you to be more present and focused on the present moment.

- **Set realistic expectations**: We can avoid unnecessary stress and disappointment by setting realistic expectations for ourselves. When faced with a setback or challenge, it can be tempting to put pressure on yourself to fix the problem immediately or achieve a certain outcome. Setting realistic expectations can help you approach the situation with a more open and flexible mindset, reducing stress and increasing resilience.

In conclusion, setbacks and challenges are inevitable in life, but how we cope with them can make all the difference. By practicing mindfulness, engaging in creative expression, connecting with others, practicing self-care, practicing acceptance, setting realistic expectations, getting outside, and challenging ourselves in new ways, we can build resilience and maintain a positive outlook in the face of adversity. It's important to remember that setbacks and challenges are a natural part of life and that we are capable of learning from and growing from these experiences. By incorporating these strategies and exercises into our daily lives, we can cultivate a mindset of resilience and become better equipped to handle whatever challenges come our way.

Celebrating Progress and Small Victories

Celebrating progress and small victories is especially important when continuing a dopamine detox lifestyle that is free from addiction. By recognizing and acknowledging your progress, no matter how small, you can stay motivated and committed to living a life free from dopamineaddic tion.

For instance, if you have successfully limited your social media use to a certain amount of time that day, take a moment to celebrate this achievement and acknowledge the hard work you've put in. Similarly, if you have found new hobbies or activities that bring you joy, celebrate that too.

Continuing a dopamine detox lifestyle can be challenging, but by celebrating progress and small victories, you can stay motivated and committed to your goals. Remember, the journey is not always easy, but every small step forward is worth acknowledging and celebrating.

Making It Last: Strategies for Long-Term Success

It is essential to incorporate practical strategies for maintaining progresst omake the dopamine detox way of life last.

Creating a Plan for Self-Care and Stress Management

Consider creating a self-care and stress management plan that includes exercise, healthy eating, and relaxation techniques.

Here is a practical plan for self-care andst ress management:

- **Schedule regular exercise**: Exercise is a proven way to reduce stress and improve overall health and well-being. By scheduling regular exercise into your routine, you can make sure that you're getting the physical activity you need to feel your best. Whether you prefer to hit the gym, go for a run, or take a fitness class, find an activity that you enjoy and that fits into your schedule. To achieve maximum benefits from exercise, it's important to maintain consistency. Aim to have at least three workouts per week as part of your routine.

- **Meal planning and cooking healthy meals**: Eating a balanced, nutritious diet is essential for maintaining energy levels and reducing stress. However, it can be challenging to consistently make healthy choices without proper planning and preparation. By spending some time each week on meal planning and prepping healthy meals, you can ensure that you're eating a variety of nutrient-dense foods. This can include planning out your meals for the week, grocery shopping, chopping vegetables, or cooking in bulk. If you're short on time, consider using a meal delivery service or investing in a meal prep kit to help streamline the process.

- **Practice yoga or meditation**: Both yoga and meditation are powerful stress-reducing practices that can help calm the mind and promote relaxation. Whether you're a seasoned yogi or new to the practice, there are many resources available to help guide you through a yoga or meditation session. Guided meditation apps such as Headspace or Calm, as well as online videos that offer yoga tutorials, can provide helpful guidance in establishing a meditation or yoga practice. To get the most out of these practices, set aside dedicated time each day to practice, and try to find a quiet, peaceful space where you won't be disturbed.

- **Spend time in nature regularly**: Whether you're going for a hike in the mountains or simply taking a walk around your neighborhood park, make sure to disconnect from technology and fully immerse yourself in the natural world. Engaging in activities that promote a sense of spirituality or connection to something greater than oneself can be beneficial for overall well-being. Try to make spending time in nature a regular part of your routine, whether that means going for a walk once a week or planning a weekend camping trip.

Self-care is about finding what works for you and your unique needs. Don't be afraid to experiment with different activities and routines untily oufindw hatfe els best.

Recognizing the Value of Looking Within—Self-Reflection and Self-Awareness

Self-reflection and self-awareness play a crucial role in maintaining progressduringandaft er the dopamine detox.

WhatIsSelf-Reflection?

Self-reflection involves taking a deeper look at your thoughts, feelings, and actions in order to gain a better understanding of yourself. It's a personal journey that can help you grow and develop as a person. It involves taking a step back from your experiences and analyzing them from a more objective perspective. Self-reflection is important for dopamine detoxing because it can help you identify triggers that may lead to dopamine cravings, as well as areas for growth and development. By becoming more self-aware, you can make more intentional choices and avoid falling back into old patterns of behavior.

To continue developing self-reflection skills, consider setting aside time each day for reflection. This could involve journaling, meditating, or simply taking a few moments to reflect on your experiences. Try to approach this practice with a non-judgmental attitude, and focus on observing and analyzing your experiences without getting caught up in self-criticism or self-doubt.

WhatIsSelf-Awareness?

Understanding your own thoughts, feelings, and behaviors is an important part of self-awareness. By taking the time to reflect on yourself and your experiences, you can gain a better understanding of who you are and how you can grow as a person. It involves being attuned to your internal experiences, as well as how those experiences impact your relationships and interactions with others. Self-awareness is important for dopamine detoxing because it can help you identify patterns of behavior that may be contributing to dopamine cravings, as well as areas where you may need to set boundaries or make changes in your life.

To continue developing self-awareness skills, consider incorporating mindfulness practices into your daily routine. This could involve practicing mindfulness meditation, taking a few moments each day to tune in to your internal experiences, or engaging in activities that promote self-awareness, such as yoga or journaling. Additionally, seeking feedback from others can be a valuable way to gain insight into your own thoughts, feelings, and behaviors, and identify areas for growth and development.

Continuing Education and Personal Development

Continuing to learn and grow through education and personal development is an effective strategy for maintaining progress and making the dopamine detox way of life last. Reading books, attending workshops, or taking courses on topics related to mindfulness, emotional intelligence, or habit formation can help you stay motivated ande ngagedint he dopamine detox process.

Books, for example, can provide valuable insights, practical tips, and inspiration for personal growth and development. *Reading* can also be a form of self-care and relaxation, helping you to reduce stress and improveme ntal well-being.

Somere commended books for personal development include:

- *The Power of Now* by Ec khartTolle .

- *AtomicHabits* by Jame sCle ar.

- *Emotional Intelligence 2.0* by TravisBradbe rryandJe anGre aves.

Attending *workshops* or taking *courses* can also be a powerful way to continue learning and growing. Workshops and courses can provide structured learning opportunities and allow you to connect with others who share similar goals and interests. Whether you're interested in learning more about mindfulness, emotional intelligence, or habit formation, there are many resources available online and in-person to help you continue your personal growth journey.

In addition to expanding your knowledge and skills, continuing to learn and grow can help you maintain a growth mindset. A growth mindset is the belief that you can learn and improve through effort and experience, rather than being limited by innate abilities or fixed traits. By cultivating a growth mindset, you can stay motivated and focused on the process of personal growth, rather than being discouraged by setbacks or challenges.

Overall, incorporating strategies for continuing to learn and grow through education and personal development can help you stay motivated and engaged in the dopamine detox process, and make the way of life last.

Final Thought

Congratulations on completing your dopamine detox journey! It's important to remember that sustaining progress is just as important as the detox itself. This chapter has discussed various strategies for sustaining a dopamine detox way of life, such as developing a long-term plan, embracing a self-compassionate mindset, celebrating progress and small victories, and prioritizing self-care and stress management.

To make the dopamine detox way of life last, it's important to incorporate practical strategies into your daily routine. These include regular exercise, healthy eating, relaxation techniques, spending time in nature, engaging in activities that promote self-reflection and self-awareness, and continuingoure ducation and personal development.

Remember, setbacks and challenges are a natural part of the journey. By cultivating a mindset of resilience, embracing imperfection, and practicing self-compassion, you can overcome these obstacles and continue making progress toward a life free from dopamine addiction.

Remember to give yourself credit for every step you take towards your goals, no matter how small they may seem. Each step is a success worth celebrating, so keep pushing forward and stay committed to your journey. With a little dedication and determination, you can sustain the progress you made during the dopamine detox and continue living a healthy, fulfilling life.

Conclusion

The secret of change is to focus all of your energy, not on fighting the old, but on building th e new.—Soc rates

As we come to the end of this book, I hope that the information and insights provided have been valuable in your journey towards a healthier and happier life. The 10-Day Dopamine Detox Plan is a comprehensive guide equipped with the necessary knowledge and tools to reduce dopamine levels and improve mental health, productivity, and ove rall w ell-being.

Throughout the book, we explored the science of dopamine and how it affects our mental and emotional health. We also delved into the dangers of dopamine overload and how it can negatively impact our lives. By understanding the importance of dopamine detox, you have taken the first step toward a better life.

The practical tips and strategies in this book, including preparing for the detox, the 10-day detox process, mindfulness, exercise, healthy eating, sleep hygiene, journaling, stress management, and positive self-talk, have given you the roadmap to achieve a more balanced and fulfilling life .

I encourage you to take a moment to reflect on this experience. You may have faced challenges, but the progress you made and the insights you gained are invaluable. Celebrate the victories, even the small ones, and use any se tbacks or struggles as opportunities to learn and grow.

It is important to remember that the *10-Day Dopamine Detox Plan* is just the beginning. The lessons and strategies you learned during the detox can be applied to your daily life moving forward. By maintaining a dopamine detox lifestyle, you can continue to experience the benefits of reduced dopamine levels and improved mental and emotional health.

And as you continue on your journey toward a healthier and happier life, I invite you to share your experience with others. Your story can inspire and motivate others who may be struggling with dopamine overloadorot her mental health challenges.

If you find this book helpful, please consider leaving a review on your favorite online platform. Your feedback can help others discover the benefits of dopamine detox and taketh eir first steps towards a more balanced and fulfilling life.

In closing, I want to express my gratitude for taking the time to read this book and for committing to your health and well-being. This book has provided you with the tools and inspiration you need to achieve your goals and live the life you deserve.

Be kind to yourself, stay committed to your journey, and always believe in the power of positive change. With the right mindset and effort, you can achieve anything you set your mind to.

Socrates' timeless words of wisdom serve as a powerful reminder that change is no walk in the park. It takes courage to step out of our comfort zone, say goodbye to old habits, and open ourselves up to new experiences. It means flipping the script from dwelling on the negatives to embracing the endless possibilities of a brighter future. Above all, it requires a steadfast mindset and unwavering determination to push through the challenges and come out victorious.

References

Ackerman, C. E. (2018, July 5). *Positive mindset: How to develop a positive mental attitude.* Positive Psychology. https://positivepsychology.com/positive-mindset/

Akers, W. (2019, November 20). *Is dopamine fasting a way to fix your brain or a silicon valley fad?* Healthline. https://www.healthline.com/health-news/what-is-dopamine-fasting

Alpe Audio. (2020, November 24). *How to build sustainable habits for lifelong learning.* https://www.alpeaudio.com/post/how-to-build-sustainable-habits-for-lifelong-learning/

Annual Reviews. (2016). *Psychology of habit.* https://www.annualreviews.org/doi/10.1146/annurev-psych-122414-033417

Baer,R.A.(2015). *Mindfulness-based treatment approaches.*Else vier.

Berkeley. (2015). *Mindful breathing (greater good in action).* https://ggia.berkeley.edu/practice/mindful_breathing

Better Help. (2018). *Addiction to dopamine: How to overcome dopamine addiction.* https://www.betterhelp.com/advice/medication/dopamine-addiction-what-is-it-and-how-to-overcome-it/

Boss, J. (2022, October 12). *Five reasons why goal setting will improve your focus.* Forbes. https://www.forbes.com/sites/jeffboss/2017/01/19/5-reasons-why-goal-setting-will-improve-your-focus/?sh=bffb9bb534a0

Boud, D., Keogh, R., & Walker, D. (1985). *Reflection: Turning experience into learning.* Crafting Justice.

https://craftingjustice.files.wordpress.com/2017/04/david-boud-rosemary-keogh-david-walker-reflection_-turning-experience-into-learning-routledge-1985-pp-1-165.pdf

Busby, E. (2021, July 31). *Dopamine detox: How to lose weight by balancing yourdopamine* .Vojo.ht tps://vojo.health/dopamine-detox/

Carver-Carter, R. (2022, February 18). *Dopamine detox: What is it, how to do it and does it work?* Atlas Biomed. https://atlasbiomed.com/blog/dopamine-detox-what-is-it-how-do-you-do-it-and-does-it-work/

Catchings, C. V. (2022, August 18). *Ten stress management techniques to help you cope.* Talk Space. https://www.talkspace.com/blog/stress-management-techniques/

Chateau Recovery. (2022, February 5). *The importance of mindset in recovery.* https://www.chateaurecovery.com/the-importance-of-mindset-in-recovery

Chopra, D. (2020, July). *Five steps to setting powerful intentions.* Chopra. https://chopra.com/articles/5-steps-to-setting-powerful-intentions

Clark, C. (2020, July 14). *Staying positive in addiction recovery.* Guardian Recovery Network. https://www.guardianrecoverynetwork.com/addiction-detox-aftercare-planning/10-tips-for-staying-positive-during-drug-addiction-recovery/

Clark, D., Schumann, F., & Mostofsky, S. H. (2015). Mindful movement and skilled attention. *Frontiers in Human Neuroscience, 9.* https://doi.org/10.3389/fnhum.2015.00297

Cleveland Clinic.(2020). *Sleep basics: REM & NREM, sleep stages, good sleep habits & more.* https://my.clevelandclinic.org/health/articles/12148-sleep-basics

Cleveland Clinic. (2022). *Dopamine: What it is, function & symptoms.* https://my.clevelandclinic.org/health/articles/

Cleveland Clinic. (2022). *Dopamine deficiency: Symptoms, causes & treatment.* https://my.clevelandclinic.org/health/articles/22588-dopamine-deficiency

Conrad, B. (2021, May 31). *The role of dopamine as a neurotransmitter in the human brain.* Enzo Life Sciences. https://www.enzolifesciences.com/science-center/technotes/2018/november/the-role-of-dopamine-as-a-neurotransmitter-in-the-human-brain/

Crego, A., Yela, J. R., Gómez-Martínez, M. Á., Riesco-Matías, P., & Petisco-Rodríguez, C. (2021). Relationships between Mindfulness, Purpose in Life, Happiness, Anxiety, and Depression: Testing a Mediation Model in a Sample of Women. *International Journal of Environmental Research and Public Health, 18(3),925.* ht tps://doi.org/10.3390/ijerph18030925

Cristol, H. (2019, June 19). *What is dopamine?* WebMD. https://www.webmd.com/mental-health/what-is-dopamine

Dali, R. (2022, May 5). *How to do a dopamine detox: 7 best healthy habits.* Dr. Lauryn. https://drlauryn.com/detox/how-to-do-a-dopamine-detox-7-best-habits/

Davis, D. M., & Hayes, J. A. (2023). *What are the benefits of mindfulness?* American Psychological Association. https://www.apa.org/monitor/2012/07-08/ce-corner

Dekin, S. (2018, September 5). *Ten ways to lead a happy & healthy life in recovery.* Mission Harbor Behavioral Health. https://sbtreatment.com/blog/10-ways-lead-happy-healthy-life-recovery/

Dent, J. (2017, April 4). *Is mindfulness all it's cracked up to be?* The Sydney Morning Herald. https://www.smh.com.au/lifestyle/is-mindfulness-all-its-cracked-up-to-be-20170404-gvd9oe.html

Deprocrastination. (2020). *How to do dopamine detox the right way.* https://www.deprocrastination.co/blog/how-to-do-dopamine-detox-the-right-way

Diana, M., Gaetano Di Chiara & Pierfranco Spano. (2014). *Dopamine.* Elsevier.

Diana, M. (2011). The dopamine hypothesis of drug addiction and its potential therapeutic value. *Frontiers in Psychiatry, 2.* https://doi.org/10.3389/fpsyt.2011.00064

Donaldson, S. I., Mihaly Csikszentmihalyi, & Nakamura, J. (2011). *Appliedpos itiveps ychology.*Rout ledge.

Dreher, J.-C., & Tremblay, L. (2016). *Decision neuroscience: An integrative perspective.*Else vierSc ience.

Ellison, K. (2022, September 22). *The science of wanting: How we unhook from dopamine.* Mindful. https://www.mindful.org/the-science-of-wanting-how-we-unhook-from-dopamine/

Entrepreneur. (2015, January 17). *Consistency is the key to breaking bad habits and forming good ones.* https://www.entrepreneur.com/living/consistency-is-the-key-to-breaking-bad-habits-and-forming/241635

Esch, T. (2013, December 3). T*he neurobiology of meditation and mindfulness.* Research Gate. https://www.researchgate.net/publication/259263009_The_N eurobiology_of_Meditation_and_Mindfulness

Fletcher, J. (2021, June 29). *How to recognize a dehydration headache.* Medical News Today. https://www.medicalnewstoday.com/articles/317511

Fortaleza, M. (2020, April 21). *Dopamine detox: How boredom can reset your mind.* Medium. https://medium.com/@mikejustdoesit/dopamine-detox-how-boredom-can-reset-your-mind-9dd27f015666

Gapin, J. I., Labban, J. D., & Etnier, J. L. (2011). The effects of physical activity on attention deficit hyperactivity disorder symptoms: The evidence. *Preventive Medicine, 52,* S70–S74. https://doi.org/10.1016/j.ypmed.2011.01.022

Gardner, B., Lally, P., & Wardle, J. (2012). Making health habitual: The psychology of "habit-formation" and general practice. *British Journal of General Practice, 62(605),* 664–666. https://doi.org/10.3399/bjgp12x659466

Garrett, B., & Hough, G. (2017). *Brain & behavior.*SAGEP ublications.

Gaudiano, B. A. (2015). *Incorporating acceptance and mindfulness into the treatmentofps ychosis.*OxfordUnive rsity Press.

Gibbons, S. (2019, April 23). *Screen time is killing teens. Could entrepreneurs use screens to also help save them?* Forbes. https://www.forbes.com/sites/serenitygibbons/2018/10/02/s creen time is-killing-teens-could-entrepreneurs-use-screens-to-also-help-save-them/?sh=2961c2241ba7

Gillette, H. (2023, January 27). *What is dopamine fasting?* Psych Central. https://psychcentral.com/blog/dopamine-fasting-probably-doesnt-work-try-this-instead

Good Therapy. (2019). *Dopamine.* https://www.goodtherapy.org/blog/psychpedia/dopamine

Grinspoon, P. (2020, February 26). *Dopamine fasting: Misunderstanding science spawns a maladaptive fad.* Harvard Health. https://www.health.harvard.edu/blog/dopamine-fasting-misunderstanding-science-spawns-a-maladaptive-fad-2020022618917

Harvard Health. (2016, September 6). *Six relaxation techniques to reduce stress.* https://www.health.harvard.edu/mind-and-mood/six-relaxation-techniques-to-reduce-stress

Haynes, T. (2018, May). *Dopamine, smartphones & you: A battle for your time—science in the news.* Science in the News. https://sitn.hms.harvard.edu/flash/2018/dopamine-smartphones-battle-time/

Health Direct. (2021, November). *Dopamine.* https://www.healthdirect.gov.au/dopamine

Heth Roderick Turnquist, Luo, X., Craig Alan Byersdorfer, & Stenger, E. (2021). Beyond *Histocompatibility—Understanding the Non-MHC Determinants Shaping Transplantation Outcome and Tolerance Induction.*F rontiers Media SA.

Holland, K. (2018, October 17). *Positive self-talk: How talking to yourself is a good thing.* Healthline. https://www.healthline.com/health/positive-self-talk

Houston, E. (2019, April 9). *What is goal setting and how to do it well.* Positive Psychology. https://positivepsychology.com/goal-setting/

Hryhorczuk, C., Fulton, S., & Décarie-Spain, L. (2016, June). *Dopamine signalling adaptations by prolonged high-fat feeding.* Research Gate. https://www.researchgate.net/publication/301235149_Dopam ine_signalling_adaptations_by_prolonged_high-fat_feeding

Hunter, C., & Glover, T. (2013). *The art of self awareness and self reflection.* Theravive. https://www.theravive.com/today/post/the-art-of-self-awareness-and-self-reflection-0000005.aspx

I.G. Sarason. (2013). *Social support: Theory, research and applications.* SpringerSc ience & Business Media.

Ivtzan, I., & Lomas, T. (2016). *Mindfulness in positive psychology: the science ofme ditationandwe llbeing.*Rout ledge.

Jazaieri, H. (2023). *What is mindfulness?* Greater Good. https://greatergood.berkeley.edu/topic/mindfulness/definitio n

Jeffrey Stephen Poland, Graham, G., & Society For Philosophy And Psychology. Meeting. (2011). *Addiction and responsibility.* MIT Press.

Jiang, S., Liu, H., & Li, C. (2021). Dietary Regulation of Oxidative Stress in Chronic Metabolic Diseases. *Foods, 10(8),* 1854. https://doi.org/10.3390/foods10081854

Jones, S. (2016). *Dopamine—glutamate interactions in the Basal Ganglia.* CRC Press.

Journal Owl. (2023).*Twenty-one day dopamine detox plan with free journal prompts.* https://www.journalowl.com/blog/21-day-dopamine-detox-plan-with-free-journal-prompts

Julson, E. (2022, February 28). *Ten best ways to increase dopamine levels naturally.* Healthline. https://www.healthline.com/nutrition/how-to-increase-dopamine

Karjala, T. (2020, January 31). *The power of positive self-talk.* Forbes. https://www.forbes.com/sites/forbescoachescouncil/2020/01/31/the-power-of-positive-self-talk/?sh=42f642e33a15

Keng, S.-L., Smoski, M. J., & Robins, C. J. (2011). Effects of mindfulness on psychological health: A review of empirical studies. *Clinical Psychology Review, 31(6),* 1041–1056. https://doi.org/10.1016/j.cpr.2011.04.006

Kolb, B., & Whishaw, I. Q. (2017). *Brain & behaviour: Revisiting the classic studies.*SAGE.

Koob, G. F., & Volkow, N. D. (2016). Neurobiology of addiction: a neurocircuitry analysis. *The Lancet Psychiatry, 3(8),* 760–773. https://doi.org/10.1016/s2215-0366(16)00104-8

Krause, A. J., Simon, E. B., Mander, B. A., Greer, S. M., Saletin, J. M., Goldstein-Piekarski, A. N., & Walker, M. P. (2017). The sleep-deprived human brain. *Nature Reviews Neuroscience, 18(7),* 404–418.ht tps://doi.org/10.1038/nrn.2017.55

Krishnakumar, D., Hamblin, M. R., & Lakshmanan, S. (2015). *Meditation and yoga can modulate brain mechanisms that affect behavior and anxiety—a modern scientific perspective.* Ancient Science, 2(1), 13.ht tps://doi.org/10.14259/as.v2i1.171

Laguna Shores Recovery. (2022, January 2). *Good habits that prevent you from relapse.* https://lagunashoresrecovery.com/good-habits-that-prevent-you-from-relapse/

Lally, P., van Jaarsveld, C. H. M., Potts, H. W. W., & Wardle, J. (2009). How are habits formed: Modelling habit formation in the real world. *European Journal of Social Psychology, 40(6),* 998–1009. https://doi.org/10.1002/ejsp.674

Langshur, E. (2021a, May 19). *9 mindful habits for well-being.* Mindful. https://www.mindful.org/9-mindful-habits-for-well-being/

Langshur, E. (2021b, December 22). *How present-moment awareness can make life more meaningful.* Mindful. https://www.mindful.org/how-present-moment-awareness-can-make-life-more-meaningful/

Léa Décarie-Spain, Hryhorczuk, C., & Fulton, S. (2016, June). *Dopamine signalling adaptations by prolonged high-fat feeding.* Research Gate. https://www.researchgate.net/publication/301235149_Dopamine_signalling_adaptations_by_prolonged_high-fat_feeding

Leal Filho, W., Raath, S., Lazzarini, B., Vargas, V. R., de Souza, L., Anholon, R., Quelhas, O. L. G., Haddad, R., Klavins, M., & Orlovic, V. L. (2018). The role of transformation in learning and education for sustainability. *Journal of Cleaner Production, 199,* 286–295.ht tps://doi.org/10.1016/j.jclepro.2018.07.017

Li, Y., Wei, L., Zeng, X., & Zhu, J. (2021, February 8). *Mindfulness in ethical consumption: The mediating roles of connectedness to nature and self-control.* Research Gate. https://www.researchgate.net/publication/349119126_Mindfulness_in_ethical_consumption_the_mediating_roles_of_connectedness_to_nature_and_self-control

Lin, T.-W., & Kuo, Y.-M. (2013). Exercise benefits brain function: The monoamine connection. *Brain Sciences, 3(4),* 39–53. https://doi.org/10.3390/brainsci3010039

Loma, A. (2020, November 16). *The value and importance of consistency in recovery.* Alta Loma. https://www.altaloma.com/the-value-and-importance-of-consistency-in-recovery/

Majsiak, B. (2022, June 23). *A beginner's guide to breath work practices.* Everyday Health. https://www.everydayhealth.com/alternative-health/living-with/ways-practice-breath-focused-meditation/

Mayo Clinic. (2022). *How to stop negative self-talk.* https://www.mayoclinic.org/healthy-lifestyle/stress-management/in-depth/positive-thinking/art-20043950

Mazziotta, J. C., Toga, A. W., & Richard S.J. Frackowiak. (2000). *Brain mapping:th e disorders.* Elsevier.

McCabe, A. (2021, April 7). *Dopamine: How what we eat impacts our brain chemistry.* Nutritionist Resource. https://www.nutritionist-resource.org.uk/memberarticles/dopamine-how-what-we-eat-impacts-our-brain-chemistry

Mead, E. (2019, September 26). *What is positive self-talk?* Positive Psychology. https://positivepsychology.com/positive-self-talk/

Melzer, T. M., Manosso, L. M., Yau, S., Gil-Mohapel, J., & Brocardo, P. S. (2021). In pursuit of healthy aging: Effects of nutrition on brain function. *International Journal of Molecular Sciences, 22(9)*, 5026.ht tps://doi.org/10.3390/ijms22095026

Mental Help. (2016, January 19). *Five ways meditation positively affects the addict brain.* https://www.mentalhelp.net/blogs/5-ways-meditation-positively-affects-the-addict-brain/

Migala, J. (2022, June 24). *Six smart tips for staying hydrated throughout the day.* Everyday Health. https://www.everydayhealth.com/dehydration/smart-tips-for-staying-hydrated-throughout-the-day/

Mind. (2021). *How nature benefits mental health.* https://www.mind.org.uk/information-support/tips-for-everyday-living/nature-and-mental-health/how-nature-benefits-mental-health/

Mindful. (2023, January 6). *Getting started with mindfulness.* https://www.mindful.org/meditation/mindfulness-getting-started/

Molendijk, M., Molero, P., Ortuño Sánchez-Pedreño, F., Van der Does, W., & Angel Martínez-González, M. (2018). *Diet quality and depression risk: A systematic review and dose-response meta-analysis of prospective studies.* Journal of Affective Disorders, 226, 346–354. https://doi.org/10.1016/j.jad.2017.09.022

National Institutes of Health. (2017, June 21). *Social wellness toolkit.* https://www.nih.gov/health-information/social-wellness-toolkit

Neff, K. (2011). *Self-compassion: The proven power of being kind to yourself.* HarperCollinsP ublishers.

Nestler, E. (2005). The neurobiology of cocaine addiction. *Science & Practice Perspectives, 3(1),* 4–10. https://doi.org/10.1151/spp05314

Newman, K. M. (2020). *How journaling can help you in hard times.* Greater Good. https://greatergood.berkeley.edu/article/item/how_journaling _can_help_you_in_hard_times

NHLBI. (2022, March 24). *Healthy sleep habits.* https://www.nhlbi.nih.gov/health/sleep-deprivation/healthy-sleep-habits

NIH. (2017, May 31). *The benefits of slumber. NIH News in Health.* https://newsinhealth.nih.gov/2013/04/benefits-slumber/

Njau, T., Ngakongwa, F., Sunguya, B., Kaaya, S., & Fekadu, A. (2022). Development of a Psychological Intervention to Improve Depressive Symptoms and Enhance Adherence to Antiretroviral Therapy among Adolescents and Young People Living with HIV in Dar es Salaam Tanzania. *Healthcare, 10(12),* 2491.ht tps://doi.org/10.3390/healthcare10122491

Nortje, A. (2020, June 5). *How to practice mindfulness: 10 practical steps and tips.* Positive Psychology. https://positivepsychology.com/how-to-practice-mindfulness/

Oppland, M. (2017, April 28). *Thirteen most popular gratitude exercises & activities.* Positive Psychology. https://positivepsychology.com/gratitude-exercises/

Osmani, V., Li, L., Danieletto, M., Glicksberg, B., Dudley, J., & Mayora, O. (n.d.). *Processing of Electronic Health Records using Deep Learning: A review.* Web Archive. https://web.archive.org/web/20200913112354if_/https:/arxiv.org/ftp/arxiv/papers/1804/1804.01758.pdf

Pennebaker, J. W., & Smyth, J. M. (2016). *Opening up by writing it down: How expressive writing improves health and eases emotional pain.* The GuilfordP ress.

Pfaff, D. W., Volkow, N. D., & Rubenstein, J. L. (2022). *Neuroscience in the 21st century.*Springe rN ature.

Pietrangelo, A. (2019, November 5). *How Does Dopamine Affect the Body?* Healthline. https://www.healthline.com/health/dopamine-effects

Preedy, V. R., Ronald Ross Watson, & Martin, C. R. (2011). *Handbook ofB ehavior, Food and Nutrition.*Springe rNe w York.

Preiato, D. (2022, January 31). *Exercise and the brain: The mental health benefits of exercise.* Healthline. https://www.healthline.com/health/depression/exercise

Quote Investigator. (2013, May 28). *The secret of change is to focus all of your energy, not on fighting the old, but on building the new.* https://quoteinvestigator.com/2013/05/28/socrates-energy/

Ravi, S. (2017). Yoga Learning and Practice: Perception by Athletes Participating in Competitive Sport. *International Journal of Psycho-Educational Sciences, 6(1).* https://files.eric.ed.gov/fulltext/EJ1254693.pdf

Raypole, C. (2019, April 30). *Dopamine and addiction: Separating myths and facts.* Healthline. https://www.healthline.com/health/dopamine-addiction

Reinholz, J., Skopp, O., Breitenstein, C., Bohr, I., Winterhoff, H., & Knecht, S. (2008). Compensatory weight gain due to dopaminergic hypofunction: New evidence and own incidental observations. *Nutrition & Metabolism, 5(1),* 35. https://doi.org/10.1186/1743-7075-5-35

Robbins, T. (2019). *The one and only mental health guide your mind needs.* TonyRobbins.ht tps://www.tonyrobbins.com/mental-health/

Robinson, L. (2019, September 11). *Mindful eating.* Help Guide. https://www.helpguide.org/articles/diets/mindful-eating.htm

Rush, R. (2020, August 11). *Dopamine detox diary.* Work It Health. https://www.workithealth.com/blog/dopamine-detox-diary-beginner-level/

Sage Neuroscience Center. (2021, November 19). *Breaking the cycle: Negative thought patterns.* https://sageclinic.org/blog/negative-thoughts-depression/

Samford, L. (2021, November 9). *8 lessons learned in my journey to sustainability!* Lena Samford. https://lenasamford.com/8-lessons-learned-in-my-journey-to-sustainability/

SAMHSA. (2023). *Recovery and recovery support.* https://www.samhsa.gov/find-help/recovery

Sanchez-Villegas, A., & Martínez-González, M. A. (2013). Diet, a new target to prevent depression? *BMC Medicine, 11(1).* https://doi.org/10.1186/1741-7015-11-3

Sandoiu, A. (2017). *Unmotivated to exercise? Dopamine could be to blame.* Medical News Today. https://www.medicalnewstoday.com/articles/314978

Sandra Silva Casabianca. (2022, April 25). *Forty-six positive affirmations for anxiety relief.* Psych Central. https://psychcentral.com/anxiety/affirmations-for-anxiety

Scott, E. (2022). *How to make mindfulness your way of life.* Verywell minded. https://www.verywellmind.com/mindfulness-exercises-for-everyday-life-3145187

Scott, E. (2023). *Five Self-care practices for every area of your life.* Verywell Mind. https://www.verywellmind.com/self-care-strategies-overall-stress-reduction-3144729

Seabrook, E. M., Kern, M. L., & Rickard, N. S. (2016). *Social Networking Sites, Depression, and Anxiety: A Systematic Review.* JMIR Mental Health, 3(4), e50. https://doi.org/10.2196/mental.5842

Shah, S. (2021, June 15). *The top 15 yoga poses for stress relief: How they can help you relax.* Art of Living. https://www.artofliving.org/us-en/blog/the-top-15-yoga-poses-for-stress-relief-how-they-can-help-you-relax

Shahbazyan, M. (2010, August 17). *How to clear your mind: 14 effective ways.* WikiHow .ht tps://www.wikihow.com/Clear-Your-Mind

Share Care. (2022). *Positive-thinking exercises to undo stressful thoughts.* https://www.sharecare.com/mental-health-behavior/stress-management/reduce-stress-through-the-power-of-positive-thinking

Sharpe, J. (2022, April 24). *How to reset your brain's dopamine balance after addiction.* West Coast Recovery Centers. https://westcoastrecoverycenters.com/how-to-reset-your-brains-dopamine-balance-after-addiction/

Silvia Gatti McArthur, Pierre Michel Llorca, Tamminga, C. A., Grottick, A. J., Mark David Tricklebank, & Martel, J.-C. (2021). *DopaminergicAlte rationsinSch izophreni*a.F rontiers Media SA.

Simopoulos, A. P. (2010). *Personalized nutrition translating nutrigenetic/nutrigenomic research into dietary guidelines.* Basel

Freiburg, Br. Paris London New York, Ny Bangalore Bangkok ShanghaiSingapore Toky oSy dney Karger.

Simple home, simple life. (2017, December 29). *How a calm home helps you reach your goals.* https://www.simplehomesimplelife.com/blog/how-to-create-a-calm-home-and-become-more-mindful

Simpson, E. H., & Balsam, P. D. (2016). *Behavioral Neuroscience of Motivation.*ChamSpringe rInt ernational Publishing.

Sleep Foundation. (2009, April 17). *What is sleep hygiene?* https://www.sleepfoundation.org/sleep-hygiene

Smith, M. (2018, December 4). *Benefits of mindfulness.* Help Guide. https://www.helpguide.org/harvard/benefits-of-mindfulness.htm

Studer, B., & Knecht, S. (2016). *Motivation theory, neurobiology and applications.*Else vier.

Suni, E. (2009, April 17). *What is sleep hygiene?* Sleep Foundation. https://www.sleepfoundation.org/sleep-hygiene

Sussman, S. (2017). *Substance and behavioral addictions.* Cambridge University Press.

Sutton, J. (2018, May 14). *Five benefits of journaling for mental health.* Positive Psychology. https://positivepsychology.com/benefits-of-journaling/

Sutton, J. (2019, April 9). *What is mindfulness?* Definition, benefits & psychology. Positive Psychology. https://positivepsychology.com/what-is-mindfulness/

Sutton, J. (2020, July 15). *Why is mindfulness important?* 20+ reasons to practice today. Positive Psychology. https://positivepsychology.com/importance-of-mindfulness/

The Recovery Village Drug and Alcohol Rehab.(2022, May 7). *The importance of step-by-step goal setting in addiction recovery.*

https://www.therecoveryvillage.com/recovery/wellness/goal-setting-in-recovery/

Todd, L. (2021, June 30). *What to know about a dopamine detox.* Medical News Today. https://www.medicalnewstoday.com/articles/dopamine-detox

Torrens, K. (2017, January 16). *What is the dopamine diet?* BBC Good Food. https://www.bbcgoodfood.com/howto/guide/what-dopamine-diet

University of Rochester Medical Center. (2023). *Journaling for Mental Health.* https://www.urmc.rochester.edu/encyclopedia/content.aspx?ContentID=4552&ContentTypeID=1

Vogel, A. (2019, August 7). *The dopamine diet.* A. Vogel. https://www.avogel.co.uk/health/stress-anxiety-low-mood/feeling-low/the-dopamine-diet/

Volkow, N. D., Tomasi, D., Wang, G.-J., Telang, F., Fowler, J. S., Logan, J., Benveniste, H., Kim, R., Thanos, P. K., & Ferré, S. (2012). Evidence That Sleep Deprivation Downregulates Dopamine D2R in Ventral Striatum in the Human Brain. *The Journal of Neuroscience, 32(19),* 6711–6717. https://doi.org/10.1523/jneurosci.0045-12.2012

Volkow, N. D., Wang, G.-J., & Baler, R. D. (2011). Reward, dopamine and the control of food intake: Implications for obesity. *Trends in Cognitive Sciences, 15(1),* 37–46. https://doi.org/10.1016/j.tics.2010.11.001

Volkow, N. D., Wang, G.-J., Fowler, J. S., & Tomasi, D. (2012). Addiction Circuitry in the Human Brain. *Annual Review of Pharmacology and Toxicology, 52(1),* 321–336. https://doi.org/10.1146/annurev-pharmtox-010611-134625

Volkow, N. D., Wang, G.-J., Fowler, J. S., Tomasi, D., Telang, F., & Baler, R. (2010). Addiction: Decreased reward sensitivity and increased expectation sensitivity conspire to overwhelm the brain's control circuit. *BioEssays,* *32(9),* 748–755. https://doi.org/10.1002/bies.201000042

Watson, S. (2021, July 20). Dopamine: *The pathway to pleasure.* Harvard Health. https://www.health.harvard.edu/mind-and-mood/dopamine-the-pathway-to-pleasure

Welch, M. J. (2005). *Handbook of radiopharmaceuticals: Radiochemistry and applications.* Wiley.

Wise, R. A., & Jordan, C. J. (2021). Dopamine, behavior, and addiction. *Journal* *of* *Biomedical* *Science,* *28(1).* https://doi.org/10.1186/s12929-021-00779-7

Ximenes-da-Silva, A., & Guedes, A. (2021). *Nutrients, neurotransmitters andbraine nergetics.*F rontiers Media SA.

Yuzbay, E. (2021, October 20). *The power of introspective writing.* Medium. https://medium.com/illumination/the-power-of-journaling-4ce13b671e7a

Zakrajsek, T. D. (2022). *The new science of learning.* Stylus Publishing, LLC.